PARENTS WHO TEACH

Stories From Home and From School

Pat Sikes

CASSELL

Cassell
Wellington House
125 Strand, London WC2R 0BB

127 West 24th Street
New York NY 10011

First published 1997

British Library Cataloguing-in-Publication Data
A catalogue record for this book is available from the British Library.

Library of Congress Cataloguing-in-Publication Data

ISBN 0-304-33332-8 (hardback)
    0-304-33333-6 (paperback)

Typeset by Kenneth Burnley at Irby, Wirral, Cheshire.
Printed and bound in Great Britain by Redwood Books, Trowbridge, Wiltshire.

This book is, of course, for David, Robyn and Joby,
because if it hadn't been for them, I wouldn't have written it!

Contents

Contents

Acknowledgements

Ever since I started working on this book I have enjoyed the recurring daydream of getting to the end and writing the acknowledgements. Now that time has come and I'm not finding it at all easy to find the right words. A whole host of people have helped and supported me in various ways and I want to say a public 'Thank you' to them all. Perhaps I should not be concerned that this is going to sound a bit like an Oscar winner's acceptance speech – after all, clichés can be sincerely meant despite sounding hackneyed. So, 'Thank you' to: Andy Hargreaves, the series editor, for taking on the book in the first place and for giving me considerable encouragement as he has always done over all of the years that I've known him; to my colleagues at the Warwick Institute of Education, especially those who belong to the Social Aspects of Education Study Group; to Linda Evans, who has supported me more than I've 'supervised' her; to the parent teachers who agreed to take part in the research; to Penny Mather, Sue Bond, Sian Adams, Angie Packwood, Anne Sinclair-Taylor and Chris Husbands for their comments and criticisms; to Fr Alan Parkinson for his funny stories, love, care and absolution; to O. L. W. for favours granted; to David, Robyn, Joby, and Joan for bearing with me; and especially to Katherine Ambler, who is undoubtedly the best nanny in the world and who looked after our children for four and a half years, giving them unlimited love, care, and fun and enabling us to go to work without worry.

I had looked forward to saying 'Thank you' to Barry Troyna, my dearest friend and colleague who encouraged and supported me and whom I could always rely on for advice and constructive criticism, but he died on 9 February 1996. Here's remembering you Barry.

Series Editor's Introduction

In Britain and Australia, they call it teaching. In the United States and Canada they call it instruction. Whatever terms we use, we have come to realize in recent years that the teacher is the ultimate key to educational change and school improvement. The restructuring of schools, the composition of national and provincial curricula, the development of benchmark assessments – all these things are of little value if they do not take the teacher into account. Teachers don't merely deliver the curriculum. They develop, define it and reinterpret it too. It is what teachers think, what teachers believe and what teachers do at the level of the classroom that ultimately shapes the kind of learning that young people get. Growing appreciation of this fact is placing working with teachers and understanding teaching at the top of our research and improvement agendas.

For some reformers, improving teaching is mainly a matter of developing better teaching methods, of improving instruction. Training teachers in new classroom management skills, in active learning, co-operative learning, one-to-one counselling and the like is the main priority. These things are important, but we are also increasingly coming to understand that developing teachers and improving their teaching involves more than giving them new tricks. We are beginning to recognize that, for teachers, what goes on inside the classroom is closely related to what goes on outside it. The quality, range and flexibility of teachers' classroom work are closely tied up with their professional growth – with the way that they develop as people and as professionals.

Teachers teach in the way they do not just because of the skills they have or have not learned. The ways they teach are also grounded in their backgrounds, their biographies, in the kinds of teachers they have become. Their careers – their hopes and dreams, their opportunities and aspirations, or the frustration of these things – are also important for teachers' commitment, enthusiasm and morale. So too are relationships with their colleagues – either as supportive communities who work together in pursuit of common goals and continuous improvement, or as individuals working in isolation, with the insecurities that sometimes brings.

As we are coming to understand these wider aspects of teaching and teacher development, we are also beginning to recognize that much more than pedagogy, instruction or teaching method is at stake. Teacher development, teachers' careers, teachers' relations with their colleagues, the conditions of status, reward and leadership under which they work – all these affect the quality of what they do in the classroom.

This international series, Teacher Development, brings together some of the very best current research and writing on these aspects of teachers' lives and work. The books in the series seek to understand the wider dimensions of teachers' work, the depth of teachers' knowledge and the resources of biography and experience on which it draws, the ways that teachers' work-roles and responsibilities are changing as we restructure our schools, and so forth. In this sense, the books in the series are written for those who are involved in research on teaching, those who work in initial and in-service teacher education, those who lead and administer teachers, those who work with teachers and, not least, teachers themselves.

One important aspect of teacher development is the way in which teachers' professional work is influenced by their lives outside teaching. Many things are important here like age, gender, religion, ethnocultural identity, personal interests. One of the most important yet under-discussed influences on how many teachers teach and how they approach their teaching is their own experience of being parents. In this book, Pat Sikes discusses how being a parent affects teachers, how it changes them in important ways.

In this richly described study of a group of teachers who are also parents, Pat Sikes shows how teachers see their own child in every child they teach, and every child they teach in their own. In a very practical and personal way, being a parent shifts the moral reference points on which teachers fix their teaching. Teaching becomes more personal, more urgent – yet, as many teachers testify, at the same time it also makes them more flexible, more relaxed. None of this, Sikes argues, means that teachers who are not parents are somehow professionally less worthy; but becoming a parent and being a parent does alter teachers professionally as well as personally.

Pat Sikes brings to her study of women and men teachers who are also parents an extensive experience of investigating how teachers' lives and careers influence every aspect of their work. Like the teachers in her book, she also brings to her writing her own recent experience of becoming a parent. Sikes writes in a refreshing, even revelatory narrative here about her own experiences and emotions of parenthood and how they have changed her as a researcher of teaching and an educator of those who are preparing for the profession, Her text is unapologetically engaged and emotional. As is increasingly the case in feminist writing, the writer is personally present in what is written. Her own voice, the voices of the teacher-parents she has interviewed and the more impersonal voices of published research are skilfully and accessibly brought together in a lucid and at times moving account that teachers and managers would do well to read.

Parenthood is often seen as an interruption to teaching or a drain of time and energy away from it. Sometimes this is true – parenting is certainly no easy ride. But Sikes' book mainly shows us how parenting of all kinds adds immeasurably to teachers' professional dedication and competence. It is, in many cases, a valid form of teacher development in itself. Instead of regarding parenthood as a subtraction from professional commitment, we would do well instead to treat it as an asset, acknowledge it as career-relevant learning, and make it a subject of more deliberate professional reflection.

Pat Sikes' book points us to all these possibilities. It is in many ways a celebration of parenthood as part of professionalism, though not a romantic one. Very many teachers are also parents or will become so. This book should draw the attention of these teachers, those who manage them, and those who educate them to one of the most widespread influences on teachers' work and the positive potential that can and should be drawn from it.

ANDY HARGREAVES
January 1997

Preface
An Explanation for an Alternative Approach

Some people, on picking up and looking through this book, might be rather surprised to find that parts of it are written in a narrative, autobiographical style, rather than in the more usual academic manner. It is possible that there will be those who feel uncomfortable with such an approach. This may be because it doesn't meet their expectations for a title from this publisher or in this series, or because, to paraphrase Catherine Emihovich,[1] the passion of the subject matter is not distanced.

Some will wonder why I have chosen to write in this way. Friends, whose judgement I respect, have said that in so doing I am making myself a hostage to fortune; others have said, 'Go for it!' I recognize the problem. Emihovich[2] says that any non-traditional academic writing, and particularly that which uses a narrative style, is risky because it is clearly not, nor makes any pretence to be, 'objective' and, therefore, 'scientific'. It does not attempt to distance the everyday from the academic. There is also the important consideration, highlighted by Madeline Grumet, that 'even telling a story to a friend is a risky business; the better the friend, the riskier the business',[3] because their view of us may be damaged by what we tell and how we tell it. What they learn about us may give them a certain 'power' which they could, potentially, use to our disadvantage in professional and social arenas.

The post-modernist and post-structuralist positions are that the reality of the text lies in the interaction between the reader and the writer. On this view it is plainly not possible to know exactly how any particular reader will read any particular text. Both their interpretation and their understanding lie in the experiences and contexts of their lives. If this means that any social science texts not presented in a traditional, academic style are rejected, then so be it. This book may not be for those people.

It has been suggested[4] that women academics are more likely to be involved in writing which takes risks. One explanation for this is that traditional forms are inimical to women's preferred ways of thinking and of making sense of the world. Following on from this, they may choose to use an 'alternative' approach in order to gently distance themselves from the 'masculine viewpoint'. Another, perhaps more pragmatic, interpretation is that the majority of women have less to lose than their male counterparts because they are not, by and large, in such exalted positions. It is true that many works which do have, at least, a personal component or are more 'experimental', are written by women.[5] Some of these women were in senior positions and could be regarded as taking a risk with their academic reputations but, more significantly, most of them had had an intense experience (motherhood, writing and submitting a doctoral thesis, cancer, for example) which, for various reasons, they wanted to write about and to share. And this is also true in my case. This book arose out of my experiences: they are central to it and are, therefore, in it.

And I want to acknowledge my experiences by saying 'I' instead of remaining invisible or, at most, making vague references to 'the author'. I also want to acknowledge the part I have played in interpreting and 'giving voice' to the people who spoke to me for the research. In other words, I want to accept responsibility for what is written, and the most straightforward way of doing this seems to be to explicitly write myself in.

In a paper which considers the epistemological status of personal and autobiographical writing in the light of its increasing popularity in educational research, Morwenna Griffiths attempts to answer the concerns of students about the 'validity of using their own life-experience in thinking about theories or reflecting on their own practice. They ask whether their own experience could really count as evidence, or if it has any wider validity beyond the anecdotal.'[6] Her response is,

> Yes, because ultimately knowledge can only be produced through the careful consideration of individual experience. But be warned! Your experience is not enough on its own. You will need to use it carefully: bearing in mind relevant theory and your political position. And you will have to be prepared to reflect and re-think your understanding of the experience over time.[7]

This, as I shall elaborate in Chapter 2, is the line that I have taken.

The point that Griffiths makes about reflection and rethinking is important. As I write in Chapter 1, and have written elsewhere,[8] in coming to this research I was, in effect, returning to a theme which I had encountered over ten years previously. At that time, I was childless and parenthood did not seem to me to be of particular significance or interest when studying teachers' lives and careers. It was mentioned by the teachers I was working with but I did not ask them to elaborate as I did with topics such as their perceptions and experiences of ageing. Whilst I did refer to parenthood in my writing, I treated it as a peripheral issue, rather than as an important area in its own right.[9] I expect that, in time, my concerns will alter yet again, other things will become more pertinent to me, and I may well reappraise and reinterpret what I am doing now. At present, however, when talking to parent teachers I am consciously talking to them from the position of being a parent myself, as well as a researcher. Consequently the data that results can be considered a 'dialogic' production in that it arises out of the relationship between the parent teacher and myself, and insofar as my autobiography is woven into what I write concerning other people.[10]

Having said this, however, I must admit that I am not eager to classify my work as being of one particular type or another. It is, rather, an amalgam. It does not, for instance, fit neatly into any of the choices or categories of 'realist', 'confessional' and 'impressionistic', which Van Maanan[11] suggests are available to ethnographers for the textual organization of their work. Yet styles of writing are clearly important. As Wittgenstein noted,[12] the choice of particular grammars and vocabularies reflects the choice of a particular reality and, furthermore, choosing 'traditional' forms can be seen as contributing to the perpetuation and reproduction of an hegemony. Such a choice does avoid the risks associated with using non-traditional styles, but this can be at the cost of communicating the essentially subjective information which a writer really wants to communicate. This is the case for me, in the present instance. William Pinar identified the problem in his 1980 article, 'The Trial', when he wrote that,

> my task is to portray singularity, subjectivity, the process of self-knowing. Yet the language available to me is that of social science, a language pretending to universality and objectivity. . . . I do not know how to see or to report what I see. How can I divest myself of this language of abstraction: how to write subjectively?[13]

The question is, how can we write subjectively yet with the legitimacy commanded by 'traditional' forms? Pinar, like a growing number of others, myself included, suspects that one answer lies in auto/biographical and narrative, storied approaches. Of course, another question concerns why this legitimacy is seen as desirable, given the criticisms levelled at traditional academic writing by those searching for and advocating alternatives. Individuals would give their own idiosyncratic answers but frequently these come back to issues of power and access to channels for being heard. But things are changing and, maybe, paradigms are shifting, albeit slowly.

Returning to my decision to write in the particular way I have chosen: as I said at the beginning, I wanted to take responsibility for my work and to 'write myself in'; I also believe that the style I have used is the style in which I am best able to say what I want to say – it feels right. This is largely because it is a style which accommodates the expression of 'non unitary' subjectivity;[14] that is, the way in which people do not have a seamless unified self but are, rather, a mass of complexities, contradictions and ambiguities. It is also a style that people not acquainted with specialized academic discourse can read relatively easily and this is important to me because my intention in writing this book has not been to write exclusively for my academic colleagues. I would also like to think that teachers and parents in other professions and none, would be able to understand what I am saying, although I recognize that such an audience is difficult to reach through the channels I am using.

When I, together with Lynda Measor and Peter Woods, wrote a book about teacher careers based on life history interviews, a reviewer in the *Times*

Educational Supplement (16 May 1986) remarked that this was a book which, he thought, teachers would find interesting to read. This book did contain 'theory' but it also used a lot of verbatim quotes and it was these which did turn out to make it popular with the teachers who read it. (Although it does have to be said that these teachers usually came to the book when they were taking a higher degree course!) The reason why they liked it was because of the style in which it was written and because of the way in which they felt that they could identify with the teachers quoted and described in the text. Barone[15] suggests that the art of writing persuasive educational stories is to seduce people into identifying in some way with what they read. This identification is achieved by means of what Bruner[16] calls 'verisimilitude', and by carefully positioned blanks which readers can fill in with their own understandings, interpretations and experiences. Put in this way it all sounds very artificial and manipulative but perhaps it is not that different from other techniques of communication, or even, for that matter, from methods for evaluating research approaches themselves. As Griffiths argues,[17] Kuhn's concept of 'shared exemplars' is based on a similar premise.

The argument that using auto/biographical, storied approaches is, in some way, more 'natural' and easy to identify with, is not without its own problems. Ivor Goodson writes that 'the way we story our lives (and, therefore, the way we present ourselves for educational study, among other things) is deeply connected to story lines derived from elsewhere'.[18] Making a similar point Bloom and Munro, writing in the same volume, warn that autobiographical and narrative forms of writing may, through their literary conventions, simply reproduce patriarchal and oppressive ideologies.[19] There is no easy answer or neat way forward. Perhaps it simply has to be accepted that all we can do is use what is available and, as far as we are able, craft it to our own purposes.

Finally, I cannot, and would not wish, to dictate how people should read and make sense of what I have written. I hope some people will enjoy it and I expect others will not. I must acknowledge that, inevitably, I write from a political position, one which values the experiences of parenthood in general and motherhood in particular, and it may be that, ultimately the audience for this book lies with others who also share this conviction.

NOTES

1   Emihovich, C., 'Distancing Passion: Narratives in Social Science' in Hatch, J. A. and Wisniewski, R. (eds), *Life History and Narrative*, New York, Falmer, 1995.
2   Ibid, p. 41.
3   Grumet, M., 'The Politics of Personal Knowledge' in Withering, C. and Nodding, N. (eds), *Stories Lives Tell: Narrative and Dialogue in Education*, Columbia New York, Teachers' College Press, 1991, p. 69.
4   See, for example, Cotterill, P. and Letherby, G., 'Weaving Stories: Personal Auto/Biographies in Feminist Research', *Sociology* 27, 1, 1993, pp. 67–80 and various contributors to Withering, C. and Nodding, N. (eds), *op. cit.*, pp. 67–77.

5 See, for instance, Cotterill and Letherby, *op. cit.*; Emihovich, *op. cit.*; Griffiths, M., '(Auto)Biography and Epistemology', *Educational Review* 47, 1, 1995, pp. 75–88; Grumet, M., *Bitter Milk: Women and Teaching*, Amherst, University of Massachusetts Press, 1988; Wilkins, R., 'Taking it Personally: A Note on Emotions and Autobiography', *Sociology* 27, 1, 1993, pp. 93–100; Rose, G., *Love's Work*, London, Chatto & Windus, 1995.

6 Griffiths, *op. cit.*, p. 75.

7 Ibid, p. 87.

8 Packwood, A. and Sikes, P., 'Telling Our Stories: Adopting a Post Modern Approach to Research', *International Journal of Qualitative Studies in Education* 9, 3, 1996, pp. 1–11.

9 Sikes, P., 'The Life Cycle of the Teacher', in Ball, S. and Goodson, I. (eds), *Teachers' Lives and Careers,* Lewes, Falmer, 1985, pp. 27–60; Sikes, P., Measor, L. and Woods, P., *Teacher Careers: Crises and Continuities*, Lewes, Falmer, 1985.

10 For further discussion and examples of dialogic work see Clandinin, D., 'Developing Rhythm in Teaching: The Narrative Study of a Beginning Teacher's Personal, Practical Knowledge of Classrooms', *Curriculum Inquiry* 19, 1989, pp. 121–41; Elbaz, F., 'Knowledge and Discourse: The Evolution of Research on Teacher Thinking', in Day, C., Pope, M. and Denicolo, P. (eds), *Insight Into Teachers' Thinking,* Basingstoke, Falmer, 1990; Grumet, *op. cit.*; Personal Narratives Group, *Interpreting Women's Lives: Feminist Theory and Personal Narratives,* Bloomington, Indiana University Press, 1989; Pinar, W., *Autobiography: Politics and Sexuality: Essays in Curriculum Theory 1972-1992,* New York, Peter Lang, 1994; Tierney, W., 'Self and Identity in a Post-modern world: A Life Story', in McLaughlin, D. and Tierney, W. (eds), *Naming Silenced Lives: Personal Narratives and Processes of Educational Change,* New York, Routledge, 1993, pp. 119–34.

11 Van Maanan, J., *Tales of the Field*, Chicago, University of Chicago Press, 1988.

12 Wittgenstein, L., *Philosophical Investigations* (3rd edn), trans. G. Anscombe, New York, Macmillan (original work published in 1953).

13 Pinar, *op. cit.*, p. 43.

14 Bloom, L. and Munro, P., 'Conflicts of Selves: Non unitary Subjectivity in Women Administrators' Life History Narratives', in Hatch, J. and Wisniewski, R. (eds), *Life History and Narrative,* London, Falmer, 1995, pp. 100-101.

15 Barone, T., 'Persuasive Writings, Vigilant Readings, and Reconstructed Characters: The Paradox of Trust in Educational Storysharing', in Hatch, J. A. and Wisniewski, R. (eds), *Life History and Narrative,* New York, Falmer, 1995, pp. 63–74.

16 Bruner, J., *Actual Minds, Possible Worlds,* Cambridge MA, Harvard University Press, 1986.

17 Griffiths, *op. cit.*, p. 78.

18 Goodson, I., 'The Story So Far: Personal Knowledge and the Political', in Hatch, J. A. and Wisniewski, R. (eds), *Life History and Narrative,* New York, Falmer, 1995, p. 95.

19 Bloom and Munro, *op. cit.*, p. 111, note 6.

Chapter 1

Becoming a Mother
A 'Transformative Experience'

INTRODUCTION

It is 4 o'clock on a winter's afternoon. I am upstairs in my study, writing about the ways in which parenthood affects teachers, when Katherine, our nanny, brings Robyn, aged 4, and Joby, aged 2, home from school and nursery respectively. The children rush upstairs. Joby climbs on my knee and starts hammering the word-processor keyboard while Robyn tells me about the writing she did at school today. 'I wrote, "My mummy likes doing her work but she doesn't do any ironing."'

This is true. I have always avoided that particular task unless I or Katherine have decided it is absolutely necessary, usually two minutes before going out. Since having my children my attitude to ironing has not changed, but it has to lots of other things and it is because of these changes that this book has come about.

In common with many other women who have been in a position to write about it, having children fundamentally changed the way I saw and experienced the world.[1] My priorities shifted, my values altered. As Lewin puts it, 'becoming a mother is perceived as a transformative experience, an accomplishment that puts other achievements in their proper perspective'[2] and this is certainly how it was for me. On a professional level, the sorts of things I wanted to research also changed to take in motherhood and issues associated with it.

The only other experiences which have had anything like the same impact for me have been the deaths of people I love. I expect it is like that for most of us. Birth and death are, after all, the key life-events. However we experience them, whether personally or through people we are close to, they influence the ways in which we make sense of the world. We are interested in them and want to try to better understand what they mean for us. As academics some of us are well placed to undertake this task. Ann Oakley, for instance, invokes C. Wright Mills' injunction to deploy the sociological imagination in connecting private to public when she notes that 'academic research projects bear an intimate relationship to the researcher's life . . . personal dramas provoke ideas that generate books and research projects'.[3] For Oakley, like me, motherhood was the drama.

In recent years it has become quite common for researchers working within the 'qualitative' tradition, particularly those using ethnographic and biographical methods, to offer a reflexive account of the conduct of their research; indeed, Stephen Ball suggests that 'research biographies' should be compulsory.[4] These accounts generally involve the researcher in giving some personal details in order to situate themselves in relation to their work and, often, to describe how they came to their topic. The reason that is usually given for this is that such background information enhances the rigour of their work by making potential biases explicit. Whether or not it actually does do this is open to question.[5] In some cases there may be an element of what Mary Maynard terms 'vanity ethnography';[6] that is, when the researcher tells their story in order to indulge a desire for self-publicity, as much as, or more than, to benefit their account and analysis. It may also be true that, as Cotterill and Letherby suggest,[7] some researchers do it in the hope that introducing a personal element will protect them from criticism.

The rest of this chapter will largely consist of an autobiographical account. By recounting how I came to be researching the ways in which parenthood in general, and becoming a mother specifically, influences teachers' perceptions and experiences of their work, my intention is simply to tell the story of a particular research project which would not have happened had I not had a child of my own. In a sense therefore, my story is an extended metaphor for the research and it is for this reason that I have chosen to tell it.

MY STORY – FROM CHILDLESSNESS TO MOTHERHOOD: A CHANGING WORLD-VIEW

As far back as I can remember I did not like little children and I particularly disliked babies. I always knew why I felt this way: it was to do with jealousy. I was the much-loved only child of a couple who were not able to have any more children. This was the great sadness of my mother's life. I vividly recall the times when nosy, unthinking people would ask her if, or when, she was going to have another baby and she would say something like, 'It's not through choice there's only one. There's nothing I would like more but we've not been lucky enough.' To cope with her unhappiness she vested all her interest and love in me. I was aware of this and I did not want to share. I saw babies as a threat to my position. Once she talked to me about the possibility of adopting a child. It was before I went to school so I would have been 3 or 4. What would I think if a baby came to live with us to be a brother or sister for me? I'd like it wouldn't I? I remember being shocked to the core. I know that I was colouring something in in a picture book at the time but cannot recall if I responded with anything more than a non-committal grunt. It would have been easy enough in those days to adopt a baby but, I later learnt, my father was not keen on the idea: he didn't think he could love anyone as much as he loved me, his own child.

So I grew up, the centre of my parents' universe. The only blot, as far as I was concerned, was that I was a girl. I passionately wanted to be a boy because, it seemed to me, they had all the fun. They did all the things I wanted to do and they were everything I wanted to be. I did my best. I went and helped my dad at the iron foundry where he worked. I had my hair cut very short and was thrilled to be mistaken for a boy. I resisted 'girlish' occupations like needlework and cookery: and I hated babies and everything to do with them.

Time passed. I made my parents very proud by going to college to become a teacher. I did not have any burning desire to teach but for a 'working-class' girl (first generation to go on to higher education) who liked the idea of going to college in the town where her boyfriend was living and working as a teacher, it seemed a 'sensible' choice. Far more sensible than pursuing my idle moment fantasies of trying for a place at drama school or following up a chance to read theology at Oxford.

However, when I got to college I found that I did not really enjoy teaching practice at all. This was largely because I had little interest in, and was even a bit frightened of, the children who had the misfortune to come into contact with me. I did love the academic work though and decided that I wanted to continue with it, so when I left college I was lucky enough to go straight into an educational research job. After a year out at work I moved to another university and began full-time study for a PhD. When my studentship came to an end I did various research assistant jobs, interspersed with short periods of time working as a supply teacher, and then became a lecturer in a university.

To my surprise I had enjoyed the supply teaching because it was associated with the research I was involved in and because it was not permanent. I also found that I really liked the teaching component of my lecturing job. I put this down to the fact that I could relate much better to older students than I could to school-age children and because I was very interested in and committed to the topics and issues I was dealing with.

So by the time I was 30 I had a career and a life in which parenthood didn't feature. I was happy; my husband, David, whom I'd been with since I was 16, was happy; and my mum and dad thought the world of me.

Then, in common with many other women these days, if women's magazines are an accurate indicator, when I was about 32, I began to think about the rest of my life. If I didn't have children, would I be likely to regret it in years to come? I began to suspect that I might, although I could not put my finger on why because I still didn't have positive feelings about babies or small children. I talked to my husband about it. He said that he was happy with our life as it was but had an open mind about becoming a father.

Having raised the issue though, we found that it would not go away. Even out shopping for food we would end up discussing the merits and drawbacks of particular types of pushchair – from the point of view of potential consumers rather than that of detached observers. Thus it was that, almost imperceptibly, we came to the conclusion that we should 'try for a baby'.

But things were not as simple as they might have been. I had been ill in my early twenties and we knew that as a consequence of this it would not be an easy matter for me to become pregnant. So I started attending a 'fertility' clinic. After about six months it began to look as though the treatment would not work so we decided that we would give up and get on with enjoying our childless lives. We were not devastated by this; a bit sad, yes, but we had tried and that, to me, was the main thing.

And then, as so often happens, without any technical assistance or warning things started working and I conceived. We were thrilled by our 'success'. My parents, who had sadly reconciled themselves to never having grandchildren, were delighted. But the euphoria didn't last long because when I was about nine weeks pregnant and at a conference in Canada, I had a miscarriage.

I was upset, but more so by a feeling of personal failure than by loss. I hated telling people that I wasn't pregnant any more because I thought that they would think I was inadequate and stupid. I was also convinced that it wouldn't happen again, that it had been my one and only chance and that I had blown it. But it wasn't and by the time a couple of months had passed, I was pregnant again.

We were very excited but we kept the news to ourselves until six months and the immediate danger of miscarriage had passed. I could not bear the thought of having to tell people that I had failed again; and anyway, our relationship with this growing someone was private. For, this time, right from the start, I had a strong sense of the baby as a someone: a someone I was desperate to meet, not as a baby, but as a person.

As time went by we got to know this person better. David called it Henry. Not, he maintained, because he wanted a boy but because Henry wasn't a name we were likely to get attached to. We saw Henry when I had scans and, not being skilled at interpreting these, thought that s/he bore more than a passing resemblance to a lizard. Then I began to feel and, not long after, to see her/him moving in my stomach. Once this had started it didn't stop. From twenty-four weeks onwards Henry had the hiccups at least twice every day and, given the twisting and turning that went on, this didn't seem surprising. By now we were besotted, but not just with Henry; to our amazement we were now passionately interested in all babies and small children.

Despite this interest we knew that we were completely ignorant about how to look after a baby so we enrolled in the ante-natal classes run by the women's hospital where I was 'booked in' to give birth. These classes became the highlight of our week. The first part of the session was taken up with relaxation and breathing exercises, then came a sort of seminar on an aspect of child care or childbirth, and it was this which we found so fascinating. The midwife was a good teacher who, wherever possible, used experiential or active learning strategies. I have to say though, that I don't think she got it quite right when she asked us to put our little fingers in the corners of our mouths and pull, and then told us that this was what having a baby felt like. I noticed that the three second-time mothers in the class looked a bit sceptical, especially when she went on to say that she herself had had a caesarean delivery. But that aside, we had total confidence in what we were told.

As the weeks went by we learnt how to hold, change, dress, bathe and (demand) feed babies. We were advised about what equipment we would need, which disposable nappies were the most efficient, and how tiring it all would be. We were taken to the special care baby unit and we looked at the tiny mites, most of whom were, by this time, actually younger, in gestational terms, than Henry was. The majority of us in the class cried, for those babies and for our own.

I am sure that seeing these premature babies would have upset me before I was pregnant but I know that I wouldn't have felt it so intensely or personally. Similarly, when cases of child abuse and murder came into the news I could hardly bear to listen because I knew that such things could potentially happen to Henry. In a strange sort of way, my yet-to-be-born child was all children, and all children were my child.

Even before this child was born my world-view had changed. The way I thought had changed. Was it the hormones or some atavistic force working in me that had brought this about? I didn't then, and I don't now, have much time for the notion of 'instinct', so what was going on? In her work, Sara Ruddick suggests that caring for children, rather than being a biological parent, gives rise to 'distinctive ways of conceptualizing, ordering and valuing'.[8] She calls this philosophical stance 'maternal thinking' and argues that its key interests are related to preserving, reproducing, directing and understanding. Was I now thinking maternally? Certainly a lot of things were different and I was surprised at how far-reaching the influences were. It was even affecting how I was experiencing certain aspects of my job.

I continued to work until I was thirty-six weeks pregnant and this work involved me in going into classrooms and observing student teachers on teaching practice. I was used to some teachers and students being sarcastic, unkind and downright mean to children. This had always worried and disgusted me for the 'usual' reasons, namely that it was exploiting an unequal power relationship, was likely to have a negative effect on the children's educational, emotional and social development, was bad practice, and was straightforwardly nasty and unnecessary. Now, though, I felt such behaviour personally for Henry in the children and for the children in Henry. It could be my child in the class and I didn't want him/her, or anybody else's child, to be treated in that manner. Consequently I was less likely than I previously had been, to excuse the teacher or student because they might, for whatever reason, be having a bad day and I started, politely, asking them why they had acted or spoken as they had. The students didn't mind this because it was what they expected from me but, perhaps not surprisingly, the teachers were not impressed. Fortunately my maternity leave started before the complaints had a chance to come in!

Another part of my job was interviewing for places on the postgraduate teacher education course. There was a change here too. I now had a new criterion for judging suitability for teaching: would I like Henry to be taught by this person? When I mentioned this to co-interviewers, all those who were parents said that this was their acid test too.

Eventually the time came for my maternity leave to start. By now I was gross, suffering terrible heartburn and really longing for Henry to be born to relieve my discomfort. Every day I walked a mile to my local shops and fantasized doing this pushing a pram, but that was about as close as I got to imagining what it would be like to have the baby here. I was very superstitious. We had bought the aforementioned pram, a car seat, and various other bits of exciting equipment but I had insisted that we leave it at the shop, just in case. We also had a layette box filled with little vests and suits and similar things though again, just in case, I hadn't examined its contents. David eventually had to pack my bag for the hospital with things for me and for the baby because I was so afraid that something would go wrong.

Reading what I have written about my pregnancy it sounds as if I was in a terrible state of anxiety but it was not like that. The months spent waiting for Henry were amongst the happiest in my life: I just could not allow myself to think too far ahead.

The estimated due date (EDD in medical jargon) came. I remember that we went for a walk at a local beauty spot and met a couple from our ante-natal class. They had had their baby for a fortnight and were just discovering that the pram cramped their walking style. I looked at their son and wondered whether we would have Henry with us by the end of the day. Of course we didn't, and I went to bed fed-up.

The next day dawned. David went to work. I found that I just could not concentrate on the paper that I was trying to write so I started to do the only jigsaw puzzle we had in the house. I felt as if I was getting a cold and when my mother phoned that evening to see how I was, I told her I was ill and that it was her fault because I'd caught it from her when she'd visited the previous week. My cousin rang a bit later to ask how it was going and I told him that I thought I would still be pregnant the same time next week. I didn't want any dinner but David made me eat a baked potato and cheese, 'to keep up your strength'. Then I went to bed. My bump was so enormous that David took a photograph of it as a sort of 'wonder of the world'.

I woke up at 2 a.m. and just made it to the bathroom where I was violently sick. David had poisoned me with his bloody potato. He, however, thought my labour had started. By 4 a.m. I conceded that he might be right and we went to the hospital. Walking into the delivery room I saw the little aquarium-like cot made ready for the baby with a folded blanket and a sheet and I fervently hoped that there would be someone to put into it at the end of the day.

Henry was born two hours later at 6 o'clock. She weighed 7lb 12oz, had masses of black hair, was exquisitely beautiful, and screamed with such vigour and intensity that when we got to the maternity ward the sister said she had already been warned about her. As soon as David phoned with the news, my parents set off to come and see us and by mid-morning they had arrived. I gave Henry to my dad first of all. He was clearly enchanted and I have to confess that I felt a pang of jealousy at seeing him so taken with her. I also realized that my relationship with him and with my mum would never be quite the same again. Some people say that it is only when your parents die that you can really stop being a child. For me, at any rate, having my own child and knowing what that felt like, made me, in my own eyes, feel more responsible and grown up.

In the evening, when all the visitors had gone and Henry was sleeping in her fish tank beside me, I lay down and looked at her. She really was beautiful. She had forced her way out with great energy so she wasn't squashed or bruised as babies sometimes can be. Everyone who had seen her had marvelled at her loveliness. Suddenly I was overwhelmed with a feeling of panic. I was responsible for her and would be, God willing, for many years to come. I was petrified and convinced that I would not be able to cope.

Eventually I managed to go to sleep. It had, after all, been a long day. About five minutes into a nebulous yet disturbing dream, I was woken by loud screaming. It took a few minutes to work out where I was and where the noise was coming from but then I remembered that I was a mother. I picked Henry up, made a clumsy attempt to change her nappy and then tried to feed her. She was not having any of it. The screaming continued unabated. Finally, in desperation, after about an hour, I rang the bell for the nurse. When she came I told her that I had done everything that I could think of to stop the baby crying but none of it had worked. She looked at me and said, 'You need to do something because you're disturbing everyone. Use your instincts.' Then she turned round and went out.

I was astonished. As I said earlier, I did not subscribe to the notion of 'maternal instinct' insofar as it is taken to refer to an intuitive and involuntary prompting to do what is necessary for the well-being of the child. After all, I had gone to classes to learn how to do the most rudimentary things and everything I had learnt had been totally new to me. I suppose that, without the classes, I would have muddled through, but with considerably more stress and potential, albeit minor, damage or discomfort to the baby. The long and the short of it was that I had not got a clue so, even if there are maternal instincts more precise than a drive to protect one's child from danger, I certainly didn't have them. While I was pondering this, Henry fell asleep of her own volition.

In many ways this was the pattern for the rest of Henry's babyhood. (Perhaps I should note that when she was three days old Henry was renamed Robyn Henrietta – we could not bring ourselves to completely dispose of her eponymous identity.) I would do everything I could think of to resolve a situation and it would either work or it wouldn't. Certainly my view of the world had changed, my priorities and values had shifted, the things I did were different but I am sure that none of these changes were the result of instinctual prompting. I am not aware of doing anything in the course of looking after my child that was not the result of some sort of experience, whether my own or someone else's. Furthermore, now that I was a mother, other mothers were willing to confide that it had been the same for them, unless they had had prior experience of babies; and even then, faced with their own baby, they had been at a loss as to what to do at times. This was true of my mum, my aunts, my cousins, Maureen next door and casual acquaintances at the baby clinic. The only people who had anything to say about instinct seemed to be those without children.

I went back to work when Robyn was four months old. I didn't find it difficult to leave her because I knew that she was being well looked after and I knew that if I stayed at home I would get fed-up and bad tempered and would end up being a lousy mother. Of course, it was the case that the nature of my work and the money it provided made it possible for me to return to the work I loved. Not everyone is in this position, and not everyone wants, or feels that it is right, to leave their children.

Once again, when I went into classrooms in the course of my work, I felt a sense of my child in the children there. If anything it was stronger than it had been when I was pregnant. This was not sentimentality but rather personal concern for each child to get the best deal. Even while I was at college I would have said that I wanted this but it was different now. My concern now had flesh on its bones, it was more real because I had Robyn. I am also sure that I had changed as a teacher of intending teachers, for now I was even more concerned that they should go out and become critical and reflective practitioners who did the best for every child they taught. On a slightly different level, I don't think that my students would have been flattered to know that I saw them as somebody's children too, but I did and I think this made me less impatient at times. And I had changed in terms of my pedagogy too. I have always liked to use examples in my teaching and now I had some really good ones, and new ones at that, every day. I knew that younger students sometimes got irritated when their mature colleagues repeatedly referred to their children so I was a bit cautious and made certain that I wasn't just taking the opportunity to tell of some 'cute' behaviour or saying. I think I got the balance right because students told me that they found the examples helped them understand the theories I was teaching. Apart from anything else therefore, having my own children has made aspects of my teaching a great deal easier and possibly more effective!

When, two years later, our son Joby was born, I was quite a different person in all respects. I had a store of 'maternal experiences' to draw on and some confidence which resided in the fact that nothing too disastrous had happened to Robyn as yet. I had made some 'mistakes' though, but saw these as experiences which I could learn from, second time around. Of course Joby was quite a different character from his sister, much happier and more 'laid back', possibly partly as a result of my greater confidence, and I sometimes got it wrong with him too. But now I felt less like I was playing at mothers and more like a mother myself.

In the intervening years other things had also happened which had a significant impact on me. I had had another early miscarriage which had hurt much more, emotionally, than it had the first time because I had been much more conscious of what I was losing. Worse than this though was that my darling dad had died from lung cancer, three weeks before Joby was born. For me, having a child that my father hadn't seen was very hard and very painful. But my dad's illness and death were not just negative experiences. During his last year he had some remission from the cancer and because we knew that time was short, we deliberately did lots of things together like going to the zoo, spending days on the beach, walking through the pine woods and on the sands, and having picnics and lunches in the gardens of country pubs. These times taught me a lot, not only about death, but about life and about being a parent. They added to the changes in my thinking that had started when I became a mother. So, what does being a mother mean to me?

WHAT BEING A MOTHER MEANS TO ME

In a subsequent chapter I shall be looking at the literature which deals with conceptualizations and ideologies of parenthood but here I want to offer my own personal view.

Inevitably my views are coloured by my own experiences of mothering and of being mothered and by my observations of other mothers' mothering. Then there are the books, of various kinds, that I have read, in which motherhood has been described, defined or analysed. Social class, education, the nature of family and parental relationships, sexuality, economic circumstances, friends, religion, 'race', historical and geographical location all play their part too, along with a host of other influences too numerous to mention.

Basically, I believe that the various models of motherhood that are available at any time are social constructions and I acknowledge the implications of this belief for my views. For *me*, at the time of writing, being a mother means that I have been partially responsible for the creation of two unique and amazing people. I, very selfishly, brought them into being so I owe them everything and they owe me nothing. I have no right to be disappointed by anything in their appearance, their physical constitution, their sex or their sexuality, their intellectual aptitudes or capabilities, their mental state or the nature of their individual characters. They have the right to accept my unconditional love and the best I am able to do in consistency with my beliefs, values and circumstances, in terms of physically caring for them and preparing them physically, emotionally, morally, spiritually, educationally and intellectually for the world.

I am aware that, to some extent, this is something of a romantic view. It is also the view of a mother of *young* children. Having read what I have written about what motherhood means to me, a friend pointed out that as children get older and make increasing demands upon practically every resource their parents possess (time, money, patience, even-temperedness) and when they reject the values and beliefs they have been taught, it becomes more difficult to sustain such a view.

But even with this proviso I imagine that, in essence, my view is not very different from that held by many, perhaps the majority, of parents: what will vary is the detail. For example, different people will have different views about what constitutes appropriate educational, moral and spiritual preparation. Some parents would also disagree vehemently with my belief that someone else can look after my children better than I can while I go to work. They might feel that the fact that I do this calls into question my suitability to be a mother, because, in their view, I abdicate some of the caring to another person.

PARENTS AS TEACHERS: FINDING A FOCUS FOR RESEARCH

But what does all this have to do with teachers in schools? As I have already noted, having the children changed me as a teacher. Although this surprised me it should not really have done. The reason for this is that some years earlier I had worked on a research project which used biographical methods to study secondary-school teachers' experiences and perceptions of teaching.[9] A colleague, Lynda Measor, and I had, between us, interviewed forty teachers of various ages and at different career stages. Around three-quarters of these teachers were parents and all of them had mentioned the ways in which they believed they had changed, with regard to their work, once they had had their children. I knew about the 'phenomenon' I was experiencing, I had talked to teachers about it, I had even written about it but in some ways it did not register. The impact of parenthood had only been a tiny part of the work we were doing and we had not explored it in any detail or given it any special significance. I now think that this was because I was guilty of what Michelle Fine describes as 'othering',[10] that is, of seeing the teachers I was working with as separate, distinct and different from me. Now that I had become a mother and was aware of how significant that experience was for my professional life, the process of 'othering' was interrupted and I could hear, with clarity, what those teachers had been trying to tell me. I needed to go back and listen more carefully to what parent teachers had to say, not least in an attempt to better understand my own experiences.

I subsequently set up a research project which focused on teachers' perceptions of the ways in which parenthood had influenced all aspects of their professional lives. After almost ten years it was only possible to return to one member of the original group that we had worked with (and my meeting up with this man was entirely fortuitous) but there was no shortage of parent teachers who were willing to participate.

This book does not just tell the story of that research but rather draws on it in order to raise wider issues about the nature of teaching and parenting in a more general sense.

HOW THE BOOK IS ORGANIZED

The way in which the book is organized is as follows.

Chapter 2 considers the life history methodology which was used for the collection and analysis of data. Parenthood is clearly a major personal and social life-event and, as a consequence, a person's sense of self is likely to change in some ways. That this change may also affect their professional sense of self is at the crux of the research questions I have posed. Since it is impossible to investigate teachers' professional selves without setting these within the developing contexts of the teachers' lives as wholes, life history seemed to be the most appropriate research method to use, for it allows the life to be connected to the work in an accessible and coherent manner. In addition to discussion of methodological issues, some details about the people who took part in the research are given. Their words and experiences are then used as illustrations and examples throughout the rest of the book

Chapter 3 moves on to look at dominant conceptualizations and ideologies of parenthood. The majority of the attention is, in fact, given to motherhood, for while mothering and motherhood are topics which have attracted considerable attention from researchers and commentators representing a range of theoretical positions and working in a variety of disciplines, fathers and fatherhood have tended to be neglected. Consequently there is not the same extensive body of literature on which to draw and in which to contextualize what the father teachers had to say.

'Parenthood', 'mothering' and 'motherhood' are social constructions, and what they are understood to mean and involve is dependent upon what is going on in the particular contexts in which they are enacted. At the present time, in Western society, the dominant conceptualization, revealed and explicated in popular literature (magazines for example) and parents' manuals on child development (by authors such as Penelope Leach, Miriam Stoppard, Hugh Jolley and Benjamin Spock for example) presents an ideal model of (middle-class) mothering whereby mothers are expected to be ever vigilant and sensitive to the needs of the child which they meet in an uncontrived manner. All experiences are to be, consciously, turned into opportunities for learning. Although this model of mothering is presented as being 'natural', spontaneous and 'commonsensical', evidence suggests that it is in fact a very recent development.[11] Fathers are implicated in this approach to parenthood but the assumption is that their involvement will be to a lesser extent: their parental responsibilities are depicted as being of quite a different order.

Moving on from parenthood in general and motherhood in particular, Chapter 4 is concerned with the notion of teacher as parent. Surprisingly perhaps, given the key similarity in the relationship between adult and child, this is an area which has not traditionally been seen as a significant and important factor influencing how teachers teach. This has meant that it has rarely been considered to be a legitimate focus for academic study and research.[12] Despite this there is a literature which deals with the links between, and the similarities in, the roles of 'mother' and 'school teacher', and in particular, 'primary-school teacher'.

Benn has written that,

historically, there have always been two distinct teaching functions: the first an extension of mothering, and reserved for women; the second an extension of power and authority, reserved for men, who have guarded it well. This division – while no longer explicit – is still implicit throughout the education system.[13]

Steedman expands on this and argues that over the last 200 years a discourse of 'mother-made-conscious' has come to predominate within primary schooling.[14] This chapter explores what this discourse means for teachers, and looks at differences in the conceptualization of the roles of male and female teachers.

Chapter 5 consists of the life histories of a number of the teachers who took part in the research. These give a sense of the unity, albeit sometimes filled with contradictions, of the teachers' experiences as they relate to parenthood and their professional work. They are also 'good' stories which engage the interest and offer the reader the opportunity, should they wish to take it, to compare their own perceptions and experiences with those presented. Accounts of how individual people make sense of and live out social roles and meanings are a valuable corrective to grand, macro theorizing which, whatever it purports to do, does have a tendency to an over-generalized and deterministic view of humankind.

Following on from this, Chapter 6 makes it plain that the intention in writing this book has not been to set up iconographies of parent teacherhood in which many teachers who are parents fail to recognize their own experiences and consequently may feel diminished or undermined. As Hirsch argues with reference to mothers, we need to recognize 'difference within the feminine and multiple differences within the maternal'.[15] Nor do I wish to argue that parenthood is essential for 'good' teaching. Rather what I want to do is to acknowledge that some of the knowledge, skills and understandings which can accrue from the experience of motherhood specifically, and parenthood more generally, cannot but help to have a positive impact upon how mothers and fathers who are teachers, teach. Like Grumet I believe that it is important that we do not deny the importance of the emotional experience of parenthood because,

> by withholding information about that relation [of parent to child] from the public discourse of educational theory we deny our own experience and our own knowledge. Our silence certifies the 'system', and we become complicit with theorists and teachers who repudiate the intimacy of nurture in their own histories and in their work in education.[16]

NOTES

1   For example, Casey, K., *I Answer With My Life: Life Histories of Women Teachers Working For Social Change*, New York, Routledge, 1993; Cosslett, T., *Women Writing Childbirth: Modern Discourses of Motherhood*, Manchester, Manchester University Press, 1994; Everingham, C., *Motherhood and Modernity*, Buckingham, Open University Press, 1994; Gieves, K., 'Introduction' in Gieves, K. (ed.), *Balancing Acts: On Being a Mother*, London, Virago, 1989; Gitlin, A. and Myers, B., 'Beth's Story: The Search for the Mother Teacher'

in McLaughlin, D. and Tierney, W. (eds), *Naming Silenced Lives: Personal Narratives and Processes of Educational Change,* New York, Routledge, 1993; Grumet, M., *Bitter Milk: Women and Teaching,* Amherst, University of Massachusetts Press, 1988; Oakley, A., *From Here to Maternity: Becoming a Mother,* Harmondsworth, Penguin, 1979; Treblicot, J. (ed.), *Mothering: Essays in Feminist Theory,* Maryland, Rowman & Littlefield, 1983.

2   Lewin, E., 'Negotiating Lesbian Motherhood: The Dialectics of Resistance and Accommodation' in Glenn, E., Chang, G. and Forcey, L. (eds), *Mothering: Ideology, Experience and Agency,* New York, Routledge, 1994, p. 348.

3   Oakley, *op. cit.,* p. 4.

4   Ball, S., 'Self-doubt and Soft-data: Social and Technical Trajectories in Ethnographic Fieldwork', *International Journal of Qualitative Studies in Education* 3, 2, 1990, p. 170.

5   See Troyna, B., 'Blind Faith? Empowerment and Educational Research', *International Studies in the Sociology of Education* 4, 1, 1994, pp. 3–24.

6   Maynard, M., 'Feminism and the possibilities of a postmodern research practice', *British Journal of Sociology of Education* 14, 3, 1993, p. 329.

7   Cotterill, P. and Letherby, G., 'Weaving Stories: Personal Auto/Biographies in Feminist Research', *Sociology* 27, 1, 1993, pp. 67–80.

8   Ruddick, S., 'Maternal Thinking' in Treblicott, J. (ed.), *Mothering: Essays in Feminist Theory,* Maryland, Rowman & Littlefield, 1983, p. 224.

9   Sikes, P., Measor, I. and Woods, P., *Teacher Careers: Crises and Continuities,* Lewes, Falmer, 1985.

10 Fine, M., 'Working the Hyphens: Reinventing the Self and Other in Qualitative Research', in Denzin, N. and Lincoln, Y. (eds), *The Handbook of Qualitative Research,* London, Sage, 1994.

11 Helterline, M., 'The Emergence of Modern Motherhood: Motherhood in England, 1899–1959', *International Journal of Women's Studies* 3, 6, 1980, pp. 590–615.

12 Exceptions are: Casey, K., 'Teacher as Mother: Curriculum Theorizing in the Life Histories of Contemporary Women Teachers', *Cambridge Journal of Education* 20, 3, 1990, pp. 301–20; Grumet, *op. cit.*; Martin, J., *Reclaiming a Conversation: The Ideal of the Educated Woman,* New Haven, Yale University Press, 1985.

13 Benn, C., 'Preface' in DeLyon, H. and Widdowson Migniuolo, F. (eds), *Women Teachers: Issues and Experiences,* Milton Keynes, Open University Press, 1989, p. xix.

14 Steedman, C., 'The Mother Made Conscious: The Historical Development of a Primary School Pedagogy' in Woodhead, M. and McGrath, A. (eds), *Family, School and Society* Milton Keynes, Open University Press, 1988.

15 Hirsch, M., *The Mother/Daughter Plot: Narrative, Psychoanalysis, Feminism,* Bloomington, Indiana University Press, 1989.

16 Grumet, *op. cit.,* p. xvi.

Chapter 2

Stories and Lives
Life History and Parent Teachers

IDENTIFYING AN APPROPRIATE RESEARCH APPROACH

As a result of what had happened to me, I wanted to investigate if and how becoming a parent had affected other teachers' perceptions and experiences of their professional lives. Goodson writes that 'in understanding something so intensely personal as teaching it is critical we know about the person the teacher is'.[1] Elaborating on this theme, Nias has claimed that 'the self is a crucial element in the way teachers themselves construe the nature of their job'.[2] Becoming a parent is a major personal and social life-event which is likely to provoke changes in a person's sense of self. My study, therefore, demanded a focus on individual parent teachers' senses of self within the various social worlds they inhabited. This is because, within these social worlds, roles and concepts such as 'mother', 'father', 'parent', 'teacher', 'professional', 'personal', 'career', have particular meanings, carry different identities and involve different experiences which are dependent upon how people are socially positioned. For example, being identified as a 'black, single mother', a 'good Catholic mother', a 'working mother', a 'primary-school teacher', or a 'divorced father' means being subject to certain expectations and being perceived and treated in particular ways by other people. This has implications for people's social relationships and also for the quality of their lives in a practical as well as an emotional sense.

Gaining access to parent teachers' interpretations, understandings and experiences was, therefore, crucial. Consequently the questions that needed to be asked concerned such things as: how they understood and constructed 'motherhood' and 'fatherhood'; what becoming a parent had meant for them in their lives in general and with regard to their professional lives in particular; what their priorities and values were; how they saw and experienced their role as teacher, and how this informed and was informed by, and how it articulated with, their views about parenthood.

Underlying and implicit to the identification and prioritization of these questions is a symbolic interactionist view of the world which involves conceptualizations of lives as multi-faceted; of social and personal constructions of meanings and, therefore, of identities; and, consequently, of language and discourse as the conveyors and media of meaning.[3] Whilst acknowledging the importance of individual, subjective interpretations of experience and understandings, the significance of the influence that social context has upon these interpretations has to be recognized. For example, as shall be argued later, certain discourses and ideologies of mothering have been dominant at particular historical times and have shaped individual mothers' perceptions, understandings and experiences of motherhood. Like Cosslett I find myself caught in the dilemma of 'wanting to affirm [individuals'] voices, the inscription of their hitherto marginalised subjectivities, and needing to show how these voices, these subjectivities have been culturally constructed by prevailing discourses and cultural practices'.[4] The goal, therefore, is to credibly depict the integration of the micro and macro domains of social life at a particular historical time.

Given both what I wanted to find out, and my interactionist perspective, a narrative and biographical research approach seemed likely to be the most productive way forward.[5] It also seemed especially appropriate since I had come to the topic through my own biographical experiences or, to put it in another way, through a process of 'heuristic inquiry'.

HEURISTIC INQUIRY

According to Moustakis heuristic inquiry involves:

> a process of internal search through which one discovers the nature and meaning of experience . . . the self of the researcher is present throughout the process, and while understanding the phenomenon with increasing depth, the researcher also experiences growing self-awareness and self-knowledge.[6]

Advocates of heuristic research[7] suggest that it consists of six phases, the first of which is 'initial engagement', that is, the discovery of an experiential issue of intense personal interest, which also holds important meanings for others in similar social situations. The autobiographical account given in Chapter 1 describes my experience of this: of how I 'discovered' the influence that being a mother was having on me as a teacher. The next four phases, 'immersion', 'incubation', 'illumination', and 'explication', variously involve the researcher in both actively enquiring into, and reflecting on, the issue and also in being open and receptive to tacit knowledge and intuition. The process culminates in the 'creative synthesis', usually in narrative form, of all the themes and dimensions that have been identified.

Heuristic strategies are useful in that they explicitly recognize personal knowledge and experience as valid and valuable data. However, they are less useful, to my mind, when presented as a sequential and linear process which must be followed precisely. I would suggest that research is rarely, or never, so neat, and that, in reality, researchers move in and out of the various stages in a recursive manner. Thus, while I can classify my experiences of research in terms of the identified phases of heuristic inquiry, I cannot honestly claim to have kept to the prescribed pattern. And I also did other things because it is important, in my view, to match methodology to the situation and the issues and questions being investigated. Appropriateness should always be the prime criterion and, if an eclectic mix of methods seems likely to be most productive, then this is what should be used. Nevertheless, it must be accepted that, as a result of their biographies, researchers conceptualize the situations they research in different ways and pose research questions which reflect this. Consequently particular methods will seem more suitable to them than others. Hence the need to recognize 'the reflexive character of social research'[8] and to reflect upon the research process.

Following on this injunction, my intention in this chapter is to consider biographical and narrative research approaches and some issues around their use in my particular investigation. It is important to do this given the way in which research methods colour the nature and content of the data they yield. Without having some insight into why a particular approach is chosen and how it is used, readers are only in partial possession of the information they need in order to make sense of what is written.

USING BIOGRAPHICAL AND NARRATIVE APPROACHES IN EDUCATIONAL RESEARCH

Biographical approaches can involve a number of specific types of data including biography, autobiography, diaries, and written and oral accounts. They can be concerned with lives in their entirety or particular events in, or aspects of, them. I have used a 'life history' approach, that is, I have collected stories told by teachers who are parents about how they believe having children has altered them and has had implications of various kinds for their work. These stories have then been analysed in the light of other evidence. Goodson describes this approach in the following way:

> The crucial focus for life history work is to locate the teacher's own life story alongside a broader contextual analysis, to tell in Stenhouse's words 'a story of action, within a theory of context'. The distinction between the life story and the life history is therefore absolutely basic. The life story is the 'story we tell about our life'; the life history is a collaborative venture, reviewing a wider range of evidence. The life story teller and another (or others) collaborate in developing this wider account by interviews and discussions and by scrutiny of texts and contexts. The life history is the life story located within its historical context.[9]

Consequently I have considered what mother teachers have to say in the light of dominant ideologies of mothering and motherhood and, therefore, in terms of their gendered identities and experiences. I have done the same, with additional reference to 'fathering', for the few male teachers who participated.

Similarly teachers' thinking about their practice and their professional philosophies has been situated in the context of historical trends in education prevalent at different times during their careers. Inevitably individual life stories brought to the fore other potential influences on personal experience and sense of self, especially in relation to being a mother or father and a teacher, which needed to be considered. These included experiences of racism, of membership of various socio-economic and socio-cultural groups, of particular religious and doctrinal backgrounds, and of being adoptive rather than 'birth' parents. All of these factors together with relevant social, economic, educational and historical factors have to contribute to contextual analysis.

It is also essential to take into account informants' own interpretations and analyses of their understandings and the things which have happened to them. Goodson talks of life history being a collaborative research strategy; indeed, the business of telling and hearing life stories only makes sense if it is conceived of as being a joint action. Stories mean nothing on their own. What gives them their meanings are the 'interactions which emerge around story telling'[10] and these interactions include the interpretations made by tellers and hearers. My request for people to talk to me about the ways in which parenthood had influenced their professional life was also an explicit invitation to analyse how having their own children might have changed them as teachers. I needed to know what they thought. To disregard their analysis when making mine would have negated the fundamental reason for undertaking the investigation in the first place.

The chief values of taking a life history approach for my investigation lay, therefore, in its capacity: first, to accommodate and make use of data produced through heuristic inquiry; second, to explicitly recognize that lives are not hermetically compartmentalized into, for example, a work self and a mother self; third, to acknowledge the crucial relationship between individuals and historical and social circumstances; and fourth, to provide evidence to show how individuals experience, create and make sense of the rules and roles of the social worlds in which they live.

In 1985 my colleagues and I wrote, 'life histories do not present themselves to us as a fully-fledged method ready for use. There is, as yet, no substantial body of methodological literature to support life history studies.'[11] Since that time, the appearance of a considerable number of journal articles, books and conference papers discussing or reporting the use of biographical methods in all fields of social enquiry, makes our suggestion that the approach, 'popular amongst "the Chicago school", but largely out of fashion since, is due for a rebirth',[12] seem prophetic. Indeed it no longer feels as necessary as it once did to justify 'qualitative' methods and especially biographical and narrative approaches with their particular emphasis on the subjective, as appropriate for researching aspects and issues of education and schooling.[13]

The increasing popularity of biographical and narrative research undoubtedly owes a great deal to the development of post-modern and post-structural thinking. Feminists have also played a major part in raising the profile of such methods, and some issues associated with their contribution will be considered later in the chapter.

Privileging individual experiences and voices (as post-modernism, post-structuralism and some forms of feminist research are inclined to do) does, of course, carry the potential consequence of slipping into a state of relativism in which any interpretation is as valid as any other. There are obvious dangers in this. The rise of narcissistic, vanity-led research was mentioned in the previous chapter, and while this trend does have some negative implications for the development of methodology, these are, perhaps, of less significance than the consequences of 'a retreat to personal emotions and interpersonal processes . . . at the cost of addressing important moral, social and political purposes outside the personal domain'.[14] Individual voices do need to be socially and historically contextualized if this is to be avoided. Hargreaves suggests that if this is done and if the limits of individual 'power' are recognized, biographical approaches can be of value, both for personal and professional development and also in terms of the conventional research goals of advancing knowledge and understanding.

Yet, despite their more frequent use and apparent acceptance as legitimate research methods, some commentators have sounded a note of caution. Troyna, for example, writes that there is

> a view which is already entrenched and circulating widely in the populist circles . . . that qualitative research is subjective, value laden and, therefore, unscientific and invalid, in contrast to quantitative research, which meets the criteria of being objective, value-free, scientific and, therefore valid . . . the question of credibility is one which, unfortunately, cannot be wished away.[15]

This is, undoubtedly, the case, even though the 'objective' status of quantitative and 'scientific' research is no longer as inviolate as it once was. Clough, for instance, taking an admittedly extreme view, argues that 'all factual representations of reality, even statistical representations, are narratively constructed'.[16]

In response to Troyna's argument it is easy to say that the tenets and criteria of positivist science are invalid, therefore credibility in terms of them is spurious. Taking this position can lead to a sort of double-bind situation because, as Hargreaves points out, in order to overthrow 'reason' it is necessary to use the tools of 'reason': to deny the existence of foundational knowledge requires foundational knowledge, and, to assert the end of uncertainties involves certainty![17] My view is to say that, once again, it depends upon appropriateness given the situation under investigation. As my research was concerned with subjective interpretations and understandings, evaluating the data I collected with reference to criteria concerned with 'objectivity' would have been inappropriate. Rejecting the positivist scientific approach is not, however, an excuse for 'sloppy' work and is not an exemption from the need to be rigorous in data collection and analysis, or to reflect critically upon the conduct of the research. Such practices would seem to be fundamental to 'good' research. What does however, need to be borne in mind is that, as ideas about what constitutes a valid area for research change, paradigms shift and methods appropriate to, and adequate for, the collection and analysis of different sorts of data also change. Without the willingness to be open to new ways of thinking or to adapt and make changes in the light of new empirical evidence, our knowledge about how the world works seems unlikely to advance.

BIOGRAPHICAL RESEARCH AND FEMINIST CONCERNS

In recent years the development of feminism has led to changes of the kind described above. Feminist writers, theoreticians and methodologists have criticized all aspects of social science for being androcentric, that is, for being based on male concerns and experiences and for reflecting a male view of the world.[18] Following on from this, a case has been made for a specifically feminist methodology yielding feminist knowledge. Although there is no consensus on what this means or what exact form it should take, common features are: a focus on women's experiences and perceptions with the consequent call for feminist theory to be derived from experience;[19] an emphasis on the importance of non-exploitative and non-hierarchical relationships with respondents;[20] research that is 'empowering' and 'emancipatory' for participants; recognition of the need for researchers to be reflexive; and an acknowledgement of the importance of emotion in the research process and in the development of sociological understanding.[21] Given these 'requirements' it is perhaps not surprising that biographical approaches have been popular with feminists.[22] However, the ways in which some feminists have used such methods and the claims that they have made for them do raise certain questions. As this book is concerned with what is often regarded as being predominantly a 'woman's issue', i.e. being a mother, and because I am writing it out of a feminist concern to acknowledge and give publicity to the influence that being a parent has on teachers' professional practice, it seems appropriate to spend a short time considering some of these.

A major criticism centres around the significance that has been accorded to personal experience in much feminist research. Obviously, accounts of women's personal experience are essential if dominant interpretations are to be challenged but, as was said earlier, these must be contextualized otherwise the picture that is presented can be determinist and essentialist. It is also the case that personal stories can seem trivial and fictional, fabrications which 'don't reveal the past as it actually was'.[23] For me at least, the purpose of using stories is not to offer 'objective truths', but rather to present very specific and contextualized personal truths which are, in themselves, understood through detailed contextual interpretation. This interpretation takes account, not only of the content of the stories, but also of the influences which have led to them being told in particular ways. As Plummer notes, 'to sense the importance of stories in social life is never to suggest that stories are all there is: the telling and reading of stories is always grounded in social processes that by definition are "beyond the stories". There is more, much more, to life than stories.'[24] Some feminist work has not, at least not explicitly, taken this line but rather has regarded experience as an end in itself.[25] Initially perhaps, in the early days of feminism (i.e. from the mid-1960s) this was sufficient because it was necessary to make personal experiences public in order both to give them validity and to politicize them as women's issues. Public as well as individual consciousness raising was essential if things were to change. However, now that it is clear that women are not a homogeneous group, and that their experiences depend upon influences resulting from their social class, sexuality, ethnicity, religion, age, etc., analysis has to proceed from a wider basis than the purely personal if it is to offer alternative and useful ways of understanding how people experience the world and what the social implications of their experiences and understandings are.

Another area of concern relates to some feminists' use of interviewing in biographical, and other types of qualitative, research. It has been frequently claimed that being a respondent in such work is to participate in a meeting of equals. Although feminists are not the only researchers to make this claim, it has become something of what Kelly, Burton and Regan call a 'key "definer" of feminist research'.[26] And yet, if the purpose of a life-story interview is to provide a researcher with data which *they* want then there is an inevitable difference in the balance of power. As Glesne and Peshkin put it, 'in most instances . . . the researcher maintains a dominant role that reflects his or her definition of the inquiry purposes. As long as the purposes are his or her own, the researcher sustains a power imbalance that may or may not get redressed.'[27]

It could be argued that attempts to reconceptualize research in order to avoid this imbalance are idealistic and that they result in unrealistic claims for the methods and approaches said to achieve these ends. Having said this, it is also true that there are other kinds of imbalance which may turn out to be more significant for both the researcher and the researched. For a start, and to a greater or lesser extent, it is the interviewee who is in control of, or, to put it another way, who has power over, what they actually tell. Then it is sometimes the case that researchers interview people who are in some way or another in a more powerful position than they are. This may or may not be a consequence of the focus and nature of the research. As Carol Smart argues, assuming that the power imbalance in the research situation is basically in favour of the researcher is 'only explicable if we ignore all social class divisions and the structures of dominance in society outside the academic world of research'.[28] Consequently any woman interviewing any man could, on one level, be considered to be in an inferior position, although given the complexity of social relations and positioning this would be a simplistic view to take. Making equalitarianism a requirement of feminist research clearly limits its scope and, ironically, its usefulness to women.[29] Yet, as Neal notes,[30] this point has tended to continue to be obscured.

The debate around equalitarianism hinges on the relationship between interviewer and respondent. If researchers are to collect 'good' life stories from their informants then the quality of the relationships they establish with those informants is crucial. 'Reciprocity',[31] which occurs when the female interviewer shares personal information with the female informant, is regarded as good feminist practice,[32] because it is believed to result in interviews which are less exploitative and hierarchical than those where the interviewer just asks the questions. Sharing information in order to be, or to appear to be, less exploitative can be seen to be instrumental and manipulative rather than socially supportive, nor does it get away from the fundamental question of who is sharing with whom. As Ann Phoenix writes,

> while it is sometimes very comfortable to be a feminist researcher inter-
> viewing women, that cosiness does not simply come from shared gender but
> is often partly the result of shared social class and/or shared colour. The
> interview relationship is partly dependent on the relative positions of
> investigators and informants in the social formation. Simply being women
> discussing 'women's issues' in the context of a research interview is not suf-
> ficient for the establishment of rapport and the seamless flow of an inter-
> view.[33]

Adherence to a 'pure' notion of reciprocity limits the scope of feminist research because it pre-empts the possibility of interviewing men. Finally, and in my view most importantly, it is essential to remember that when it comes to interviewing, the key factor which usually determines how successful the encounter will be both in terms of the data it yields and as a social interaction, is how the two people get on. Reciprocity with someone you don't like is impossible, regardless of their sex.

An issue closely associated with that of the relationship between researcher and informant is that of feminist research as an 'emancipatory' or 'empowering' experience for participants. Once again, claims of this kind are not unique to feminist researchers, although it has become something of a feminist orthodoxy. Seeking to change, or suggesting that it is possible to change, lives for the better through participation in a research project reflects grandiose, if naïve, ambitions,[34] and, at the same time, contradicts the often associated requirement that the relationship between researchers and informants should be non-hierarchical. The emphasis on equal relationships is particularly surprising given that informants in 'emancipatory' or 'empowering' projects are so often people with relatively little social power, people who have few opportunities to make their voices heard. Women, clearly, come into this category, although it should be noted that some women have more opportunities than some men do, to make their voices heard. For example, as a female academic I am able to 'speak' to more people than my father, who worked in a foundry, could.

Biographical work has been said to have empowering potential for women because it allows their voices to be heard, but everything depends on who hears them. I would agree, however, that interviews which focus on a life story can, potentially, aid personal and professional development and can lead to positive life changes. This is because the reflection that is involved may lead people to consider the things which have happened to them in a new light, which may have the effect of opening up new possibilities.[35] If this happens the research could, perhaps, be considered to be empowering, although it does not necessarily get rid of the issues around the nature of the relationship between the two parties. Indeed, it may be that it is most likely to be when a relationship is 'unequal', although collaborative, that 'empowerment' or 'emancipation' takes place. Lather, for example, talks about research as praxis, research which 'seeks emancipatory knowledge (which) increases awareness of the contradictions hidden or distorted by everyday understandings'.[36] Such contradictions need to be pointed out by someone who has knowledge of them!

BIOGRAPHICAL APPROACHES, STORY AND LANGUAGE

On the morning that I was writing this section I received a letter from an ex-student. She wrote,

> As for my news – well you guessed rightly – I am six months pregnant and still waiting to bloom! All I have is big boobs and a sore back so far but I hope the joys of motherhood will hit me post-labour or even during labour, who knows. Please pray all goes well. . . . I'm glad you are enjoying your two kids – I remember when Robyn was born – I'm sure you did a seminar with her on your lap! I can't wait to be a mum, irresponsible and impatient, I hope the kiddie doesn't suffer too much, I'd like lots more! (Mind you – depends how awful that dreaded labour's going to be. . . .)

Here is one version of a woman's story in which she tells the news of her pregnancy. It is short but it carries considerable and specific meaning. The story is told in a certain way because it is addressed to a specific reader. As that reader I have interpreted what she says in a particular way and I am relatively confident that I have understood it in the way that was intended. Ayesha writes to me both as her ex-tutor and as a fellow mother – 'I'm glad you are enjoying your two kids – I remember when Robyn was born – I'm sure you did a seminar with her on your lap! I can't wait to be a mum.' She is not finding pregnancy all that it is sometimes cracked up to be, 'I am six months pregnant and still waiting to bloom! All I have is big boobs and a sore back so far but I hope the joys of motherhood will hit me post-labour or even during labour, who knows.' Even so the prospect of motherhood clearly excites her and she has an idea of the sort of mother she thinks she will be, 'irresponsible and impatient'. Here she is comparing the sort of mum she anticipates being with an idealized mother who is neither irresponsible or impatient; she expects to be a 'deviant'. Despite her excitement she does have some concerns about the birth itself, 'Please pray all goes well. . . . I'd like lots more! (Mind you – depends how awful that dreaded labour's going to be. . . .)', and, albeit expressed flippantly, about her expected style of motherhood, 'I hope the kiddie doesn't suffer too much.'

Ayesha is doing what many pregnant women do, that is, telling her story and sharing her thoughts and concerns with someone else who has been through it all before. An English colloquial expression for pregnancy is 'to be in the club' and in some ways this is a very apt phrase. Members of a club share experiences and what they say to each other carries specific meanings which serve to reaffirm both those experiences and their membership. However, although pregnancy, childbirth and motherhood are universal to women, their experiences of these states is not. Variables such as 'race', sexuality, socio-economic status, religion, prevailing obstetric ideology and practice, and the physical and emotional state of the mother lead to many differences and it is essential that this is remembered and that different stories are told. If this does not happen iconographies are established and those whose experiences are not reflected in them are excluded.

But to return to the story. Telling and listening to stories is an important form of communication; most of us are involved in it most of the time. We create, tell and listen to stories about the things which happen to ourselves and to other people in order to make sense of them and also to impose a sense of order and linearity on what was experienced as chaotic and inconsequential. Stories offer scripts, or patterns, for us to follow in our own lives. They give events and experiences meanings, make connections between apparent contradictions, and while they may not provide a solution, they offer some sort of an explanation. They let us know that we are not alone, that other people have gone through the same things and have felt like we have. Stories also allow us to present ourselves, our experiences and beliefs as we would wish them to be presented; they allow us to create identities and correct 'reality'. We rehearse and tell stories which are especially important to us over and over again, and we may have different versions for different audiences and different purposes.

The stories which are available for us to tell, to hear, and to use as exemplars change over time depending on historical contexts. Plummer[37] writes about the way in which certain sexual stories such as stories about 'coming out', rape, sexual harassment, and child abuse have only relatively recently come to be told and heard, as a result of social changes. Bringing these stories into the public arena gives substance and status to the experiences and emotions they describe and, as Plummer argues, this can be 'empowering' on both a personal and a social level.[38] The same is true for stories about any other area of life, including teaching and motherhood. Recognizing the political potential of stories Ostriker calls upon mothers to tell theirs:

> If the woman artist has been trained to believe that the activities of motherhood are trivial, tangential to the main issues of life, irrelevant to the great themes of literature, she should untrain herself. The training is misogynist, it projects and perpetuates systems of thought and feeling which prefer violence and death to love and birth, and it is a lie. . . . The writer who is a mother should, I think, record everything she can: make notes, keep journals, take photographs, use a tape recorder, and remind herself that there is a subject of incalculably vast significance to humanity, about which virtually nothing is known because writers have not been mothers. . . . As our knowledge begins to accumulate, we can imagine what it would signify to all women, and men, to live in a culture where childbirth and mothering occupied the kind of position that sex and romantic love have occupied in literature and art for the last 500 years, or the kind of position that warfare has occupied since literature began.[39]

As in art and literature, so in research in the social sciences!

Biographical research in general and life history work in particular, explicitly depends upon stories: as data, in analysis, and in presentation. Such explicit dependency demands that certain questions are raised. These concern the relationship between the stories and the events, experiences and feelings they portray; the nature of their telling and the language that is used; and the role of the researcher in analysis and interpretation. These questions will now be briefly addressed. Before going on to this it should be noted that as a result of the influence of certain feminist and post-modern epistemologists there is now substantial support for the idea that these questions are just as pertinent for other types of research, including traditional positivist scientific work, and that 'research' should in itself be viewed as a narrative process.[40]

THE RELATIONSHIP BETWEEN STORIES AND THE EVENTS, EXPERIENCES AND FEELINGS THEY PORTRAY

This relationship is by no means straightforward but one thing is clear and that is that stories can only represent, or offer an interpretation of, experiences. Words cannot be taken to be the experiences themselves yet there is always a danger that this will happen, especially once they are written down and thereby given a sense of permanence and status.

At a relatively simple level it is clear that memory can be mistaken and that hindsight can be brought to bear upon events. People lie or offer distorted accounts, and details can be omitted or added. Different versions are told to different people in different circumstances. This happens for various reasons but the result is the same and that is that people's various life stories do not provide objective 'truths' about 'reality'. Rather, 'they give us instead the truth of our experiences'.[41] But nor is this straightforward. As Maynard and Purvis note,

> The notion of experience needs to be problematized, since individuals do not necessarily possess sufficient knowledge to explain everything about their lives. Accounts will vary depending on such factors as where respondents are socially positioned, memory etc. There is no such thing as 'raw' or authentic experience which is unmediated by interpretation.[42]

Techniques of triangulation can be used to obtain other insights and information, and contextualization adds further layers of meaning but it has to be accepted that it is impossible to 'know' in any absolute sense the reality of individual psychic reality.[43] This is because, 'unlike the Truth of the scientific ideal, the truths of personal narratives are neither open to proof nor self-evident. We come to understand them only through interpretation, paying careful attention to the contexts that shape their creation and to the world views that inform them.'[44]

Interpretations can change at both social and individual levels. Meanings are not fixed because they are context-dependent and different people interpret them differently too. Plummer makes this point forcefully when he writes about the ways in which individuals interpret and make sense of the stories which they hear and read:

> sometimes they are brought to outrage and sometimes to better understanding ... sometimes (the story) is a tool kit and manual for guidance and sometimes it is a source where people can literally find themselves in the text. Sometimes a text is read in relative isolation and sometimes it is read through a social world or an imagined community – of class, of race, of gender, of experience, of taste. Sometimes people hear so lightly what others say so intensely, and sometimes people hear so intensely what others say so lightly.[45]

This helps to explain why I 'othered' the parent teachers I worked with before my own children were born, why I did not hear what they were saying about how parenthood had affected them as teachers. Once I belonged to the 'community of parents' I began to hear those things intensely too. Despite this common membership I cannot absolutely know what being a parent teacher was like for any of my informants. I only have their stories and the awareness that what they tell me is a representation and an interpretation. I can, however, situate what they say in the circumstances in which they say it, with reference to such things as dominant ideologies of motherhood, how they are socially positioned, their age and beliefs, and so on. Doing this allows me to at least consider whether parent teachers do share some of the feelings and experiences that led me to undertake this project.

THE TELLING OF STORIES

The production and construction of stories, the ways in which they are told and the language that is used in the telling, is as important as their content. Kathleen Casey writes that 'the principal value of oral history is that its information comes complete with evaluations, explanations and theories, with selectivities and silences, which are intrinsic to its representation of reality',[46] although, as was said above, the nature of that 'reality' is not unproblematic. However, the point which Casey makes, about the way in which life stories are told, is important. Informants tell their stories for particular purposes to particular audiences. Consciously and unconsciously they make use of devices to direct interest, emphasise importance, establish common ground, and so on. Storytellers draw on what have variously been described as 'generic plots',[47] 'generalised pictures',[48] 'pre-existing story-lines',[49] or 'prior scripts'.[50] These not only provide a structure for the actual telling of stories, they can also influence people's perceptions and experiences of whatever it is that the story concerns. Plummer[51] for instance, talks about how gays' and lesbians' stories of 'coming out' can influence and shape an individual's experiences of revealing their sexuality. Similarly Cortazzi speculates about the extent to which, having heard stories about 'naughty children' and 'awkward parents', teachers subsequently categorize and experience the children and parents that they meet according to these characterizations.[52]

Pre-existing storylines also affect the ways in which people view and experience research. Participating in a research project is a specific social situation and involves certain expectations for all parties. Goodson[53] suggests that people's ideas about research, and interviews in particular, are further influenced by what they know from storylines derived from television and newspapers. Most researchers who use interviews are used to informants asking if they are talking about the 'right' sort of things because they are eager to tell the 'right' story. What respondents are doing here is turning themselves into 'socially organised biographical objects'[54] who are telling their story in a particular way for a particular purpose. This inevitably raises questions about 'truth'. For the life historian concerned with subjective understandings, the 'right' story can only be the one that is told, situated within its particular context.

The words people use to tell their stories are related to that context. Casey suggests that, not surprisingly, 'important common verbal patterns do emerge within the narratives of each particular social group of teachers in particular social circumstances'.[55] Words reveal the influence of dominant ideologies, of professional groupings, of social class experiences and so on. I was interested to find out whether parent teachers shared a common vocabulary and if so, to investigate its roots.

THE ROLE OF THE RESEARCHER

In writing up research, researchers are telling a story. Traditionally, in the supposed interests of rhetorical 'objectivity', the convention has been to excise the researcher from the text.[56] Doing this denies their role as story tellers and as interpreters, of the area they are investigating, of the literature they cite, of the data they collect, and of the arguments they advance. Throughout this book my intention is to try and acknowledge my consciousness of this. Describing the way in which I came to be involved in the research is part of this as are my attempts to convey what biographical research means to me. Now, after doing life history work for the best part of twenty years, the methodology is very much a part of my history and also of my identity. In certain contexts I describe myself as a life historian, but I almost always describe myself as a mother. These two 'selves' are central to my story and to my presentation of this work.

MY APPROACH: WHAT I DID

Once I had decided that I wanted to investigate mother teachers' perceptions and experiences of their work using a life history approach, I set about recruiting informants. As a lecturer working in a department of education I had no difficulty in gaining access to teachers and consequently the first people I approached were colleagues, students, ex-students and teachers in schools I visited on school practice supervision. Subsequently friends and acquaintances were included. As is so often the case, the sample snowballed. I would talk with someone and they would suggest that I talk to someone they knew, and so on. In the end I had more offers than I was able to take up.

Initially I only approached mothers because my primary interest lay in considering their perceptions and experiences in the light of dominant ideologies concerning motherhood and the role of women as teachers. Later on I decided to include a few fathers, primarily out of interest in what they had to say in the light of the mothers' views. Subsequently I found that I was interested in their perceptions and experiences in their own right. I also began to feel that direct comparisons were not necessarily appropriate or helpful (although I have to confess that I succumbed to the temptation to make them). To date, relatively little is known, or rather, is recorded, about fathers' experiences and perceptions of parenthood so any work concerned with them has to be on quite a different basis to that with mothers: this is certainly the case in this book although I hope to do more research into this area in the future.

Parent teachers were eager to talk with me primarily as a result of the topic. Informants themselves talked in terms of my project providing them with a voice to 'name their silenced lives'.[57] They believed that being a parent did influence how they were as teachers but that this influence was not afforded the official recognition they felt it deserved.

Inevitably the people who took part felt that they had something to say about the topic, although this did not always mean that they necessarily believed that their own view was valid. 'I don't know if this is relevant' was a frequent preface! They cannot, in any sense, be considered to constitute a 'random' sample of parent teachers but I do not believe that such a sample could be obtained. Apart from anything else, life history research demands a certain level of articulateness and a willingness to be reflective. In any case, I am making no claims for comprehensive generalization.

Although randomization was not a goal, I was concerned to speak with parent teachers with different experiences both of parenting and of teaching. Consequently the sample included people of different ages, and from different ethnic, religious and socio-economic groups. Some were single parents, although the majority had a partner. Family size varied from one to four children and one woman had adopted her child after many years of unsuccessfully trying to conceive. As teachers the informants were at different stages of their careers and some were still students. Most of the people in this latter group were 'mature' students and I decided to include them, partly because, as their tutor, I had easy access to them but mainly because in the seminars which formed part of their course they were very outspoken about the influence they felt that being a parent had upon them as teachers. The experienced teachers worked in a variety of institutions: nurseries, primary, secondary, state, and independent schools, colleges of further education and universities were all represented. Most of the participants were working or completing their initial teacher education at the time of the study. Exceptions were a couple of women who were at home with their children and a full-time masters degree student who was on sabbatical leave from her native Pakistan.

Informants came to the project through three routes: through an individual approach from me, through the suggestion of a friend, and following lectures on life history that I gave to MA groups as part of a research methods course. When I approached potential informants, simply because I knew they had children, I told them that I was doing some work on how some people, myself included, had found that becoming a parent had changed the way in which they experienced and perceived their work as teachers. I then asked if they would be interested in taking part and explained that it would involve one or more interview-conversations. Those who came via a friend had already heard about the project and they approached me saying that they would like to take part. Similarly the volunteers from the research methods course also knew what it was all about because I had talked about the work in my life history lecture. I consider myself to have been extremely fortunate and privileged to have got so willing and informative a research population so effortlessly.

The interviews proceeded according to a pattern. First I would ask if it was all right to use a tape recorder solely for my own purposes, so that I could concentrate on what was said. That there were no refusals did not surprise me. I suspect that these days tape recorders are seen as such an integral and normal part of research interviews that few people question their use. Having got permission to record I reiterated what I was interested in then asked them to tell me about their background, how they had come to be a teacher, where having children fitted in and if and how this had changed them as teachers. I also enquired about their philosophies as mothers and fathers and as teachers: what did they see as their job at home and at school and where did they think their ideas came from.

People spoke with very little prompting. I only intervened to ask questions for clarification, to lead into another area, to answer direct questions, to invite reflection and analysis, or to share experiences. Although I was not deliberately using 'reciprocity' as a research technique there was quite a bit of it and I think this was inevitable given the topic we were talking about. In my experience most parents are ever ready to talk about their children and to hear how other parents have coped with particular experiences. Mothers are supposed to be particularly addicted to talk of this kind but, having been directly asked to talk about their children, I did not notice that the fathers were any different. This sharing of experience did have implications for the relationship between me and the informants, especially, perhaps, in the case of those who were students. As I was their tutor I was definitely in a 'superior' position to them and it is possible (though knowing them, unlikely) that they were concerned that my view of them as a result of what they told me, might compromise their success on the course. However, with regard to my position as a parent compared to theirs, they were definitely more experienced. Their children were, without exception, older than mine. They had had to cope with more and had already been through most of what I had to come. This aside, they all knew that they had the information that I wanted and, because of their familiarity with research in general as a result of their own higher and professional education, were aware that this gave them 'power' in our relationship. Perhaps of greater importance though was the fact that most of the informants knew, or knew about, me and could, therefore, hopefully trust me to treat what they had to say responsibly.

When I was talking with parents whose experiences were very different to my own, especially parents from different ethnic, cultural or socio-economic groups, I could not assume the same basic taken-for-granted knowledge or ways of seeing things. We did have parenthood in common and so there were many points of similarity but there were things I did not know and had to be told. Sometimes I asked for clarification, at other times explanations were given as an integral part of the story. For instance, Nicola, married to a colonel and a member of an 'upper middle-class' family, quite rightly felt it necessary to explain to me what the life of a high ranking army wife involved, in terms of the sorts of things she was and was not expected to do and the attitudes and values she was expected to hold. Obtaining such information is all part of the necessary contextualization that must always be taking place as an integral part of the research process. There seems to be little point in research which is concerned with how particular groups of people perceive and experience the world, which does not also attend to their particular systems of meaning. And yet there are those who maintain that it is impossible for 'outsiders' to do research within particular communities. According to this view men cannot research women, whites cannot research 'blacks', straights cannot research gays, people without children cannot research parents, and so on, because the outsiders do not possess the necessary knowledge to make sense of the world as it is for insiders. A major problem with this view is that it erroneously assumes common experiences and ways of seeing within groups. It also implies that the researcher can take mutual understanding for granted. Much more convincing, from a rigorous research perspective, is an approach which borrows from Weber's concept of 'verstehen' in an attempt to empathetically understand the world as it is for other people rather than as it appears to the researcher. Such an approach is capable of picking up idiosyncrasies as well as commonalities and reveals the way in which people belong to the wider society as well as to their own particular groups. Of course, taking this approach does not mean that 'outsider' researchers will not still have to overcome suspicion or work hard to establish their credentials but they should be prepared to do these things as a matter of course in any research project .

When it came to analysis, informants again played a major part. As part of their stories they would, as was noted earlier, offer reflections, explanations, observations and theories. I also took my ideas back to them for consideration and validation. It was interesting to see that, as I had suspected, although each individual had their own story, we also had a shared vocabulary and way of talking about being parents and teachers. It is at this point that it is possible to discern the individual in the social context; to hear, for example, mothers who are teachers talking about being 'mothers' and 'teachers': that is, to hear individuals articulate their interpretations and realizations of the ideologies of mothering and teaching to which they have variously been exposed. The part that these ideologies play comes across in the commonalities, in the collective voice which also reflects the experiences which are common to mother teachers. Of course there is a variety of collective voices, each dependent upon shared characteristics or experiences. My concern has been with the shared experiences of parenting, and in particular mothering, and teaching, but within this focus I have also paid attention to individual experiences and perceptions, as well as collective voices arising from other shared social characteristics such as ethnic group and social class. Analysis, therefore, has not been about establishing objective 'truths', but rather has been concerned to look at the consequences of living and telling a particular story under particular circumstances.

THE PARENT TEACHERS: WHO THEY WERE

As the rest of the book is based on what the parent teachers have to say it is appropriate to give readers some idea of who these people were. Consequently this section contains brief descriptions of the twenty-five informants as they were at the time of the research. However, by the time the book came to be published, some details had, of course, changed. It was hard to decide what information to give in order to satisfy possible curiosities. In the end I chose to include age, ethnic group, self-defined social class, number of children, marital status, and the type of educational institution in which they worked.

Helen. Aged 32; white English; lower middle-class origins; two children aged 3 and 2, and thirty-six weeks pregnant with her third child; married to an Anglo-Catholic curate; primary-school teacher, presently at home bringing up her children.

Abida. Aged 47; Pakistani; upper middle-class origins; two children aged 27 and 22; married; she had had a varied teaching career within the independent sector of her home country which had included secondary age range teaching in a convent, being the head teacher of her own nursery, and helping to set up teacher training for independent school teachers; presently studying for an MA in Education at a British university.

Jane. Aged 44; white English; working-class origins; one child aged 15; married, although she had spent some years as a single parent when her first husband left her just after their son was born; nursery teacher in a state school.

Karen. Aged 42; white English; working-class origins; two children aged 18 and 15; head teacher of a primary school.

Rebecca. Aged 46; white English; middle-class origins; one child aged 15; married; lecturer in an FE college.

Lesley. Aged 39; white English; working-class origins; two children aged 6 and 8; married; lecturer in a university.

Janice. Aged 49; white English; middle-class origins; three children aged 25, 22 and 19; married; independent-school teacher.

Jo. Aged 40; white English; working-class origins; two children aged 4 and 6; married; university lecturer.

Doreen. Aged 41 ; white English; middle-class origins; two children aged 13 and 10; married; student teacher.

Katie. Aged 37; white English; working-class origins; three children aged 12, 10 and 8; married; student teacher.

Teresa. Aged 22; Afro-Caribbean, lived all her life in England; working-class origins; one child aged 4; single; student teacher.

Nicola. Aged 34; white English; upper middle-class; one adopted child aged 6; married; student teacher.

Liz. Aged 32; white English; working-class origins; two children aged 7 and 5; married; student teacher.

Margaret. Aged 28; white English; working-class origins; two children aged 10 and 5; separated; primary-school teacher.

Sylvia. Aged 49; white English; middle-class origins; two children aged 22 and 18; married; head teacher of a nursery, infant and junior school.

Gillian. Aged 32; white English; middle-class origins; two children aged 3 and five months; married; chemistry/science teacher in a secondary school; presently on maternity leave.

Margery. Aged 49; white English; middle-class origins; two children aged 23 and 19; married; chemistry/science teacher in a secondary school.

Jenny. Aged 30; white English; middle-class origins; one child aged 2; married; biology/science teacher in a secondary school.

Ann. Aged 38; white English; middle-class origins; two children aged 17 and 14; divorced; art teacher in a secondary school.

Stuart. Aged 46; white English; middle-class origins; two children aged 5 and 3; married; deputy head teacher of a secondary school.

Dennis. Aged 42; white English; middle-class origins; one child living, aged 20, one child who died, aged 10; married; head of science in a secondary school.

Brian. Aged 44; white English; working-class origins; four children aged 17, 14, 12, and 7; married; head of art in a secondary school.

James. Aged 38; white English; middle-class origins; two children, a step-son aged 13 and a daughter aged 5; married; part-time science teacher in a secondary school.

Chris. Aged 40; white English; working-class origins; three children aged 11, 10, and 4; married; art teacher in a secondary school.

Ian. Aged 42; white English; middle-class origins; two children aged 8 and 12; married; head teacher of a primary school.

NOTES

1 Goodson, I., 'Life History and the Study of Schooling', *Interchange* 11, 4, 1981, p. 69.

2 Nias, J., *Primary Teachers Talking: A Study of Teaching as Work,* London, Routledge, 1989, p. 13.

3 For a comprehensive discussion of symbolic interactionism, see Plummer, K., *Symbolic Interactionism: Volumes 1 and 2,* Aldershot, Edward Elgar Reference, 1991.

4 Cosslett, T., *Women Writing Childbirth: Modern Discourses of Motherhood,* Manchester, Manchester University Press, 1994, p. 3.

5 Plummer, K., 'Herbert Blumer and the Life History Tradition', *Symbolic Interactionism* 11, 2, 1990, pp. 125–44.

6 Moustakis, C., *Heuristic Research: Design, Methodology and Applications,* Newbury Park, Sage, 1990, p. 9.

7 Moustakis, *op. cit.*; Patton, M., *Qualitative Evaluation and Research Methods* (2nd ed.), Newbury Park, Sage, 1990; Polyani, M., *The Tacit Dimension,* New York, Doubleday, 1983.

8 Hammersley, M. and Atkinson, P., *Ethnography: Principles in Practice,* London, Routledge, 1989, p. 14.

9 Goodson, I., 'Studying Teachers' Lives: An Emergent Field of Inquiry' in Goodson, I. (ed.), *Studying Teachers' Lives,* London, Routledge, 1992, p. 6.

10 Plummer, K., *Telling Sexual Stories: Power, Change and Social Worlds,* London, Routledge, 1995, p. 20.

11 Sikes, P., Measor, L. and Woods, P., *Teacher Careers: Crises and Continuities,* Lewes, Falmer, 1985, p. 14.

12 Ibid, p. 13.

13 See Casey, K., *I Answer With My Life: Life Histories of Women Teachers Working For Social Change,* New York, Routledge, 1993, pp. 7–28; Denzin, N. and Lincoln, Y. (eds), *Handbook of Qualitative Research,* California, Sage, 1994; Maines, D., 'Narrative's Moment and Sociology's Phenomena: Toward a Narrative Sociology', *Sociological Quarterly* 34, 1, 1993, pp. 17–38.

14 Hargreaves, A., *Changing Teachers, Changing Times: Teachers' Work and Culture in the Postmodern Age,* London, Cassell, 1994, p. 74.

15 Troyna, B., 'Blind Faith? Empowerment and Educational Research', *International Studies in the Sociology of Education* 4, 1, 1994, p. 9.

16 Clough, P., *The End(s) of Ethnography,* London, Sage, 1992, p. 2.

17 Hargreaves, *op. cit.*, 1994, p. 40.

18 See, for example, Fonow, M. and Cook, J., *Beyond Methodology: Feminist Scholarship as Lived Research,* Bloomington, Indiana University Press, 1991; Stanley, L. and Wise, S., *Breaking Out Again: Feminist Ontology and Epistemology,* London, Routledge, 1983; Maynard, M. and Purvis, J. (eds), *Researching Women's Lives from a Feminist Perspective,* London, Taylor & Francis, 1994.

19 Cf. Cotterill, P. and Letherby, G., 'Weaving Stories: Personal Auto/Biographies in Feminist Research', *Sociology* 27, 1, 1993, pp. 67–80.

20 Cf. Oakley, A., 'Interviewing Women – A Contradiction in Terms' in Roberts, H. (ed.), *Doing Feminist Research,* London, Routledge, 1981; Ramazanoglu, C., 'On Feminist Methodology: Male Reason Vs Female Empowerment', *Sociology* 26, 2, 1992; Stanley and Wise, *op. cit.*

21 Cf. Jaggar, A., 'Love and Knowledge: Emotion in Feminist Epistemology' in Jaggar, A. and Bordo, S. (eds), *Gender / Body / Knowledge: Feminist Reconstructions of Being and Knowing,* New Brunswick, Rutgers University Press, 1989; Wilkins, R., 'Taking it Personally: A Note on Emotions and Autobiography', *Sociology* 27, 1, 1993, pp. 93–100.

22   Cf. Bloom, L. and Munro, P., 'Conflicts of Selves: Non unitary Subjectivity in Women
     Administrators' Life History Narratives' in Hatch, J. and Wisniewski, R. (eds), *Life Histo-
     ry and Narrative,* London, Falmer, 1995, pp. 99–112; Casey, K., *I Answer With My Life:
     Life Histories of Women Teachers Working For Social Change,* New York, Routledge, 1993;
     Cotterill and Letherby, *op. cit.*; Griffiths, M., '(Auto)Biography and Epistemology' *Educa-
     tional Review 47,* 1, 1995, pp. 75–88; Middleton, S., 'Developing A Radical Pedagogy' in
     Goodson, I. (ed.), *Studying Teachers' Lives,* London, Routledge, 1992; Personal Narratives
     Group, *Interpreting Women's Lives: Feminist Theory and Personal Narratives,* Blooming-
     ton, Indiana University Press, 1989.
23   Personal Narratives Group, *op. cit.*, p. 261.
24   Plummer, *op. cit.*, p. 167.
25   Kelly, L., Burton, S. and Regan, L., 'Researching Women's Lives or Studying Women's
     Oppression? Reflections on What Constitutes Feminist Research' in Maynard, M. and
     Purvis, J. (eds), *Researching Women's Lives from a Feminist Perspective,* London, Taylor &
     Francis, 1994, pp. 29–30; Maynard and Purvis (eds), *op. cit.*, pp. 5–7.
26   Kelly, Burton and Regan, *op. cit.*, p. 36.
27   Glesne, C. and Peshkin, A., *Becoming Qualitative Researchers: An Introduction,* New
     York, Longman, 1992, p. 82.
28   Smart, C., *The Ties That Bind: Law, Marriage and the Reproduction of Patriarchal Rela-
     tions,* London, Routledge & Kegan Paul, 1984, p. 157.
29   Stanley and Wise, *op. cit.*
30   Neal, S., 'Researching Powerful People from a Feminist and Anti-racist Perspective: A
     Note on Gender, Collusion and Marginality', *British Educational Research Journal,* 21, 4,
     1995, p. 520.
31   Oakley, *op. cit.*
32   Cosslett, *op. cit.*; Nielsen, J. (ed.), *Feminist Research Methods, Exemplary Readings in the
     Social Sciences,* London, Westview Press, 1990; Stanley, L., *Feminist Praxis, Research,
     Theory and Epistemology in Feminist Sociology,* London, Routledge, 1990.
33   Phoenix, A., 'Practising Feminist Research: The Intersection of Gender and "Race" in the
     Research Process' in Maynard, M. and Purvis, J. (eds), *Researching Women's Lives from a
     Feminist Perspective,* London, Taylor & Francis, 1994, p. 50.
34   Troyna, *op. cit.*
35   Cf. Sikes, P. and Aspinwall, K., 'Time to Reflect: Biographical Study, Personal Insight and
     Professional Development', in Young, A. and Collin, R. (eds), *Interpreting Career:
     Hermeneutical Studies of Lives in Context,* Westport, Connecticut, Praeger, 1992; Sikes, P.
     and Troyna, B., 'True Stories: A Case Study in the Use of Life History in Initial Teacher
     Education', *Educational Review 43,* 1, 1991, p. 7; Sikes, P., Troyna, B. and Goodson, I.,
     'Talking About Teachers: A Conversation About Life History', *Taboo: The Journal of Cul-
     ture and Education,* Vol. 1, Spring 1996.
36   Lather, P., 'Research As Praxis', *Harvard Educational Review 56,* 3, 1986, p. 260.
37   Plummer, *op. cit.*
38   Ibid, p. 27.
39   Ostriker, A., *Writing Like a Woman,* Ann Arbor, University of Michigan Press, 1983, p.
     131.
40   Nash, C. (ed.), *Narrative in Culture: The Use of Storytelling in the Sciences, Philosophy
     and Culture,* London, Routledge, 1990; Packwood, A. and Sikes, P., 'Telling Our Stories:
     Adopting a Post Modern Approach to Research' *International Journal of Qualitative
     Studies in Education 9,* 3, 1996.
41   Personal Narratives Group, *op. cit.*, p. 261.
42   Maynard, M. and Purvis, J., 'Doing Feminist Research' in Maynard and Purvis, *op. cit.*,
     1994, pp. 1–9.
43   Evans, M., 'Reading Lives: How the Personal Might Be Social', *Sociology 27,* 1, 1993, p. 8.

44   Personal Narratives Group, *op. cit.*, p. 261.

45   Plummer, *op. cit.*, p. 21.

46   Casey, K., *I Answer With My Life: Life Histories of Women Teachers Working For Social Change,* New York, Routledge, 1993, pp. 13–14.

47   Plummer, *op. cit.*, pp. 54–56.

48   Cortazzi, M., *Primary Teaching How It Is: A Narrative Account,* London, David Fulton, 1991, p. 13.

49   Passerini, L., *Fascism in Popular Memory: The Cultural Experience of the Turin Working Class,* Cambridge, Cambridge University Press, 1987.

50   Goodson, I., 'The Story So Far: Personal Knowledge and the Political', in Hatch, J. A. and Wisniewski, R. (eds), *Life History and Narrative,* New York, Falmer, 1995, p. 95.

51   Plummer, *op. cit.*

52   Cortazzi, *op. cit.*, p. 13.

53   Goodson, *op. cit.*, p. 95.

54   Plummer, *op. cit.*, p. 34.

55   Casey, *op. cit.*, p. 26.

56   Cf. Emihovich, C., 'Distancing Passion: Narratives in Social Science', in Hatch, J. A. and Wisniewski, R. (eds), *Life History and Narrative,* New York, Falmer, 1995, p. 42.

57   McLaughlin, D. and Tierney, W. (eds), *Naming Silenced Lives: Personal Narratives and Processes of Educational Change,* New York, Routledge, 1993.

Chapter 3

Being a Parent
What Does It Mean?

INTRODUCTION

In this chapter the focus is on parenthood and, in particular, on dominant conceptualizations of mothering and motherhood. Such conceptualizations have far-reaching and significant implications for how women view and experience mothering, and for the expectations and perceptions that other people have of women who are mothers. These experiences and perceptions still apply when mothers go out to work in paid employment. Indeed, in some respects their salience may even increase because, as shall be argued, mothers who work are not conforming to the 'ideal' model of motherhood. Consequently the following discussion is of central relevance to any consideration of mothers who are also teachers. Furthermore, as the next chapter will examine in detail, there are fundamental links between mothering and teaching (especially primary-school teaching) as they are presently conceptualized. It is, therefore, important to explore both of these areas in order to have an informed idea of the way in which they relate to and interact with, each other.

THE SELF-DENYING MOTHER

My mum has a very definite belief in the 'normal' mother. Such mothers always put their children above themselves or anyone else, want to spend all their time with them, never criticize them in any way, can't bear to hear them cry over anything, and are only happy when they are doing something for them. Mothers are there for their children. Deviation from these precepts signifies pathology or, as mum puts it, 'oddness'. She is not alone in thinking along these lines:

> Your children have to be your top priority. They always have to come first. You have to put your own life on hold for them really. (*Liz*)

> You can't be selfish when you have children because you cannot come first. (*Jane*)

> You shouldn't have kids if they aren't going to be your prime consideration. I suppose you could say that you've really got to sacrifice yourself and your own life for them. (*Margaret*)

Some mothers, however, explicitly recognizing what selflessness of this kind can mean, do not hold quite such an extreme view:

[I don't think that you should always put your kids first] because they have to realize there are other people in the world . . . mummy's got a life as well. . . . I think my mum was a good mum but I think she always put us first and that's probably why I think she was a good mum. But I don't think it was good for her really. She didn't go to work, she had five [children], she wouldn't have had time, but I think she should have made more time for herself, which is why, perhaps, she split up from my dad, I don't know. I think you should put your children first some of the time, or perhaps most of the time, but I think you've got to make time for yourself as well. (*Gillian*)

[A 'good' mother] is somebody who has a very firm identity of her own but is willing to give absolutely everything to her children, who is willing to give up everything for her children if necessary, so that means every hour of sleep. The children come first. But at the same time you've still got a duty to yourself and through that to them, to still have your own interests, your own time, your own sense of identity, and not feel that you only exist as their mum. (*Helen*)

IDENTITY AND PARENTHOOD: BEING A PARENT, NOT A PERSON

As Helen says, being a mother can mean being defined in terms of someone else. At school the other day Danielle's mum, who I often talk with in the playground, asked me if it was I who had waved to her in town earlier in the week. She said, 'I thought to myself, I think that's Robyn's mum, but you'd gone before I could wave back.' A trivial enough incident perhaps but here are two women, both in their late 30s, one a senior nurse, the other a lecturer, who don't know each other's names and who identify each other in terms of their respective children. Being defined and identified in terms of someone else means not being seen as a person in your own right, with your own desires, hopes, aspirations, abilities, achievements, shortcomings, aptitudes, sadnesses, and so on. Sometimes it doesn't matter that this happens. We have to make sense of the people we encounter within the world in a way that is meaningful to us and often this means identifying them in relation to someone or something we know about. For instance, Alan Bennett tells a lovely story about his mam's encounter with her acquaintance, Mrs Fletcher, and a 'tall, elderly, very refined-looking feller'. This man was the poet, T. S. Eliot, but it was the fact that he was Mrs Fletcher's son-in-law, his looks and his overcoat, rather than his literary credentials which impressed Mrs Bennett.[1] Eliot's reputation, identity and self-image were not diminished by being associated with his mother-in-law and his overcoat because this was a one-off, and because Mrs Bennett, despite being the butcher's wife, was not a powerful person whose views had currency in the wider world (although her son has since made her and her sayings much more widely known). Being a mother, however, means constantly being made invisible except as so and so's mother. For some people, particularly those who long for a child, this is identity enough but for others, like Gillian, more is necessary:

> I do like being a mum and, well, this is the selfish reason: I suppose
> because we all started having children at the same time at work,
> when you were pregnant or had a child you were part of this group.
> . . . Before I was pregnant, although they were still my friends,
> because they came back to work, it was only after the second one that
> they left, because I was one of the later ones that had them, had
> Robert, they all had children, I didn't really feel that I could be part of
> what they were talking about any more, so it was nice to be part of
> this motherhood group. . . . I suppose it was mainly baby things we
> were talking about but I didn't mind talking about it with them. But
> when I'd go to play group, UGH! I suppose it's because you have other
> things in common with your friends, other than babies, whereas at
> play group, that's it really, they don't know *you*. You have another
> identity at work. You're not just a mum, you're a teacher too. It seems
> to be more about what you, as a teacher, *do*, whereas, as a mother, it's
> what you *are*. I felt it diminishes you as a person. (*Gillian*)

Acquiring an identity as a mother is an interesting and unusual process. Cosslett writes,

> Being pregnant, harbouring another inside the self, challenges our usual
> notions of identity and individuality: two people are in one body. Birth then
> further disrupts our categories as one 'individual' literally 'divides' into
> two. As Julia Kristeva puts it, 'there is this abyss that opens up between the
> body and what had been its inside. . . . Trying to think through that abyss;
> staggering vertigo. No identity holds up.'[2] As a process in time, motherhood
> puts into question a woman's sense of identity, as her body changes shape
> and splits apart, and a new social role is thrust upon her. Discontinuities
> between her self before and after birth, and in her relationship to the
> foetus/baby inside and then outside her, force reformulations of her sense of
> who she is.[3]

Although a general reformulation of identity seems likely to be experienced by the majority of women who become mothers, the mother teachers who had started their careers when they were childless were, inevitably, conscious of the process in relation to their professional lives in a way that those who had come to teaching after their children were born, were not.

38

Yes, well, I'd always thought of myself as a fairly ambitious sort of a person but I found, when I had her, that I wasn't so concerned to go to the conferences. I didn't want to put the same amount of time into my work as I had, partly because I wanted to be with her and because, quite frankly, it wouldn't have been physically possible to do it. And this took me by surprise. I hadn't expected it. I didn't think it would change me to that extent. Colleagues also had some difficulties in coming to terms with how I'd changed – those without kids that is. The others, those with children, said it was what they'd expected because it had been their experience too. But it took me some time to understand that yes, I was a mother, and in some respects I was different because of that. (*Jo*)

I became a different sort of teacher after my children were born and it took me some time to accept that. You can never be the same again because of your relationship to your child both in your own experience and in how other people see you. (*Janice*)

Clearly the identity implications are not quite the same for men who become fathers because the relationship with the child is not so intimate or immediate. Nor are the social expectations of fathers so all-encompassing of men's lives; but becoming a father does, nevertheless, confer new identities.

I felt people saw me in a different light, I think, when I had my first child. You have responsibilities which you are expected to fill, but I think there's also the thing, among other men anyway, that you've sort of proved your manhood, you're a 'proper' man. (*Dennis*)

You're expected to be more responsible. You're expected to provide the food, provide the house, those sorts of things. (*Chris*)

Obviously, one of the main differences in becoming a father or a mother does lie in the visible signs, and the experience of pregnancy. Everyone can, usually, see that a woman is with child, whereas paternity has to be attributed or claimed (although DNA testing means it can now be 'proved'). Adoption and the various assisted routes to conception that are now available (i.e. techniques involving egg and sperm donation) do make this a less straightforward matter than it once was, but for most women there comes a time when it is difficult to deny that motherhood is imminent. I managed to conceal my first successful pregnancy for six months because I was superstitiously afraid that if I told people too soon I would lose the baby. When I was carrying Joby however, slacker muscles gave the game away after four months and people started asking me when I would be starting my maternity leave!

THE NARRATIVE OF MOTHERHOOD

Pregnancy, having a baby and becoming a mother is like living through a story. In contrast to many life experiences it usually involves discernible, different and discreet progressive stages, although these are subject to later reinterpretation. The impression of being caught up in a narrative is enhanced by the various popular books and magazines dealing with pregnancy, childbirth and child care that are available. These all talk in terms of progression. Indeed, a pamphlet given out by ante-natal clinics to the vast majority of pregnant women in England is called *Emma's Diary* and it takes the reader through the eponymous heroine's pregnancy in a sequential manner. For Emma and for real women the significant point is that, as soon as the impending birth is known by others, particularly medical professionals, they become mothers and a different sort of person in and to the world. Their stories change and they are seen as different characters:

> I really didn't like it when you go to the ante-natal clinic, when they refer to you as 'mum'. Some of them talk about you as if you weren't there and some of them talk at you. I suppose it's their job and it was mainly the older ones that did it, but it really got to me. (*Margaret*)

> I think sometimes, [when you're a mother] other people think you are the lowest of the low. (*Gillian*)

> I think the parents see you differently when they know you're pregnant. I felt that people were more friendly. Perhaps because it might be easier for some of them to identify with you. And I felt that they had more respect for me as a teacher too. Even before the baby was born it was as if I had to know more about kids because I was having my own. (*Sylvia*)

> My head of department, when he knew I was pregnant, he said, 'Well, that's your chances of promotion gone because you're bound to have another and then your production will go down.' (*Jo*)

Motherhood appears, in some form, in every woman's story, simply because she is a woman. Even its absence has to be explained and accounted for. This is because having children is assumed to be a 'natural' and 'normal' part of the woman's life-cycle. Gillian, for example 'always expected to have five kids, just as my mum did'. Not all women though, are prepared to take motherhood for granted. They have plans and ambitions that involve other identities:

I definitely did not want children. I really thought as I was growing up that being at home with children, because it was either/or then, was something that I definitely didn't want to do. My mother was very happy being a mum at home, didn't ever want to do anything else, and I despised her for that. . . . I knew that was something I definitely didn't want to do. It wasn't so much the being at home with children, it was the whole pattern of life and relationships between men and women that I didn't want to get into, and I just wanted . . . to go away, be anonymous, do what I wanted to do when I wanted to do it . . . and I wouldn't say it was a substitute but I felt that if you had a job where you were working with children well, that would be enough. And it was at first. Absolutely. I had no thoughts about having children at all. I was very job-oriented, not career-oriented but vocationally oriented. . . . I was the exact opposite to my mum. (*Helen*)

When I found out I was pregnant I was absolutely suicidal. I did not want any children. It was an accident. It was an accident in the sense that G had always wanted children and I'd always said, 'Well, I'm not really keen. If you want them, OK, one day.' It was a 'one day' sort of thing, 'in the future' and it will never happen. . . . I'd always thought that if I did get pregnant it wouldn't really bother me that much. That's why I wasn't bothered about taking precautions. But when I did get pregnant, it did bother me, a hell of a lot. To the extent that early on in pregnancy, within the first three months, I started bleeding. I had this threatened miscarriage and I was cursing because I was also on study leave and I had to really cram for my finals for the BEd, which I was obsessed with, and I didn't want to end up in hospital. They were all for sending me to hospital with this threatened miscarriage. Had I not been heading for the finals then, I'd have jogged up and down and tried to have a miscarriage. Sounds awful, doesn't it? But the fact was I didn't want to go to hospital and ruin the finals. I wanted to get this bloody first [class degree] and I'd already had half the study leave in bed as it was, through morning sickness. I was absolutely furious with this baby for arriving, not only because I didn't want the damn thing but also because it was potentially that I couldn't get a first now. That was it, I'd blown it. . . . So this baby wasn't the most welcome child on earth and right up to the day when she was born, if I could have taken a pill, or said a magic word which would have got rid of it, I would have done. This was the end of my life. It was over now. (*Lesley*)

Women are also, 'naturally', expected to love their children, and by extension other children, and to have the ability to nurture them and to provide the sustenance and care they need. 'Instinct' is the means by which they are supposed to be able to accomplish this. As Gieves puts it, 'nature is expected to come to the aid of women to transform themselves from individuals into ideals'.[4] However, nature is not as 'natural' as positivist scientists would have us believe and 'natural', as it relates to motherhood, 'can easily be made to mean whatever is culturally sanctioned at the time, and, when applied to women, can be used to reinforce reactionary prescriptions about their role'.[5] In other words, mothering and motherhood are, to a large extent, socially constructed concepts, constructed in such a way as to meet certain social needs. The same is true of fatherhood, but this is generally accepted. I have seldom, if ever, heard anyone referred to as a 'natural' father but I have heard of 'good' fathers. These are men who do over and above what is expected of them in their role. It is hard to imagine a mother being seen in such a light!

At the most fundamental level, childbirth and rearing are the two most crucial social tasks there are. As a result of their biology women have to do the first, the second is much less obviously designated, although it has come to be women's responsibility. Given the importance and significance of mothering, it is not surprising that a considerable amount has been written about it, both in theoretical and in practical terms. As mothering has been the central feature in women's lives, in terms of both their experiences of being mothered and as mothers, the subject has been central to feminist theorizing.

FEMINIST VIEWS AND MOTHERS' EXPERIENCES OF MOTHERHOOD

Many feminists have argued that, in most societies, motherhood is oppressive, bad, and even dangerous for women because it defines them solely in terms of their ability to give birth: it casts them in a subordinate and restricted role 'while paying lip service to the social importance of their role'.[6] It is said to do this for all women, regardless of whether or not they have children, because those who don't are seen as defective.[7] There are those radicals, notably Shulamith Firestone,[8] who have gone so far as to suggest that women will never achieve equality with men while they are the ones who have to bear children. Others, however, have been concerned to reclaim motherhood as a positive female identity.[9] These writers have often themselves experienced the intense, description-defying subjective experience of motherhood and are,

> reluctant to give up the idea that motherhood is special. Pregnancy, birth, and breast feeding are such powerful bodily experiences, and the emotional attachment to the infant so intense, that it is difficult for women who have gone through these experiences and emotions to think that they do not constitute unique female experiences that create an unbridgeable gap between men and women.[10]

All of the women I talked with felt like this, even those who, like Lesley, were reluctant mothers. They believed that motherhood was special and that this 'specialness' constituted a sort of psychic, if not actual, 'power'. It made them different: Jane and Karen described this in the following words:

> When you've had your own there's something inside that alters. I think that motherhood alters you more than probably anything else because it's a physical thing that's happened to you. (*Jane*)

> You can read and read and read about it in books and it's as they say, once you've had your own children your life's never the same again and I think your attitudes and perceptions are never the same again. You are different. (*Karen*)

For those who, like Nicola, do not actually carry their own children, being a mother is still uniquely special:

> I wonder if the amount of time you wait for a child increases your appreciation of that child when it arrives? I still feel excited when I collect her from the child-minder (even though she is 6 now). I think, Oh, lovely. You know? (*Nicola*)

Critics claim that characterizing motherhood as special in this way does not make it any the less oppressive within society. As Glenn, again, notes,

> Even those who are highly critical of the way motherhood has been distorted by patriarchal, capitalist ideology, tend to romanticize the experience of motherhood, using the same language of naturalism that they deplore as sexist when used by anti-feminists. . . . The paradox is that, in order to claim positions of power and influence, women have to accommodate prevailing notions that women possess special knowledge or qualities by virtue of being mothers. Such claims reinforce the very ideology that justifies women's subordination, that is, the notion that women are essentially different from men and thus should be relegated to specific functions in society.[11]

This is difficult. The women I talked with did believe that they were different because they were mothers and they were glad that this was the case. They did not subjectively experience their motherhood as subordination, quite the reverse in fact. But then they were thinking at an individual level and their circumstances were not those of many other women. These teachers are 'educated'; they are articulate and assertive; most of them had made a definite choice to have children; they have interests and concerns beyond their families; most of them live in relatively 'comfortable' homes; they tend not to have financial worries; and the majority have partners who, if not positively supportive, at least tolerate what they do. They know they are more fortunate than others. Abida, in particular, felt that she had been especially favoured. Married at 18 to a husband of her parent's choosing, she recounted what happened on the morning after her wedding:

> I was very lucky with my husband. I got married to escape my home
> and in my mind at 18 decided that if I wasn't happy I'd go away, leave
> the marriage but never come back home. And then it turned out very
> well, just by chance, and the first thing my husband said when we got
> married was, 'Do exactly what you want to and just forget your
> mother. If you want to study, study. If you want to work, work. If you
> don't want to do anything, don't. I'm not going to stop you doing
> anything.' (*Abida*)

Given these options she chose to do a degree, have two children and go to work. By comparison, Margaret left her husband because he was not happy with her going to university. She was not prepared to 'be kept down'.

FATHERS' VIEWS ON FATHERING AND WORK

There is, of course, a difference between these individual women's experiences and the experiences of women in general. Within society women tend to be subordinate to men and the areas that have come to be women's special concern carry social penalties. This can be seen by looking at what some of the father teachers had to say. Like the women these men had experienced changes in their values and perceptions when they became parents. They had found that they were not as prepared to devote as much of themselves and their time to work as they had before their children were born. They were also less concerned to pursue promotion and this was just as well because they felt that their obvious commitment to their families made them seem less suitable candidates. They were experiencing the prejudice that women have always experienced, particularly prejudice in the workplace, and their masculinity was, they felt, also under question.

> Things changed after the children were born. By then I'd been a
> deputy head for about twelve years. I had been applying for headships
> for quite some time and I'd had interviews but times had changed and
> I wasn't the sort of person governors were looking for. On one level we
> could have done with moving because where we lived meant that my
> wife had an awful amount of travelling to get to her work but we
> talked about it and we decided that I'd stop applying. Obviously there
> were mixed reasons but the main one was that we both wanted me to
> be there for the kids. If you're a head you have to be out to meetings at
> night and that means you can't be at home. One of the deputies that

used to work with me got a headship and I met him on a course one day and he told me he regretted it. He said his family were suffering. His son had told him that he was going to make an appointment to see him because he never did anymore. He'd said you see more of the kids you teach than you do of me, and this had devastated Sam. But he said 'What do you do?' If you've got the job you have to do it and me being as I am I'd do it up to the hilt and I realized I just didn't want it. I wanted to be at home with the kids. . . . It was interesting though, I did apply for a temporary, one-term headship at my school and I did hear that the governors thought that I wouldn't be the right person because it was generally known that I took time off work if necessary to look after the children and because of my views about evening activities. (*Stuart*)

I know that some people find it hard to understand that I've done the bulk of the child care and that L actually earns more than me. The kids sometimes say things that make me think they regard me as a bit of an oddity, not like other men: and some of the women I teach on IT courses, they don't think it's right that I should be doing what I do. (*James*)

It's to do with time and the time you spend with people and time you spend with your kids, and the career thing, I really thought well, this is a load of rubbish. This is not what I want. . . . What's been going on here (in this school) has even more convinced me of that, even more. God! What is this? Nothing. If I could retire in five years I'd do it. . . . I was off the first term here, this year, because I had pneumonia. And if you don't do anything else you think then and I felt, well, people soon forget you. Your colleagues and things. You try to imagine you're irreplaceable in some way, like people always remember you. And the kids'll be saying, 'Where is he today?' But once you're gone other people do it, other people do that job so you're not irreplaceable like that. But you are irreplaceable to the people at home. No one could ever be what you've been to them. You can't replace that. (*Chris*)

There seems to be this view around that if you don't go after promotion, if you don't progress up the ladder then you're less of a man. (*Dennis*)

A PATRIARCHAL CONCEPTION OF MOTHERHOOD

The ways in which motherhood and child care have been socially constructed mean that they are not synonymous with 'success' in the world. This, it is argued, is because it is men's discourses and ideologies that become dominant and, as men do not bear children or take primary responsibility for their nurturance, these activities have been marginalized.

This has not happened accidentally. Gramsci's concept of 'hegemony' is useful in explaining what has gone on. Hegemony refers to the process by which 'common sense' and 'elaborated ideologies' inter-relate in such a way that supports the existing social order. Hegemony is not, however, a fixed state. It has to be worked at and it faces challenges. As Gramsci explains, 'common sense is not something rigid and immobile, but is continually transforming itself, enriching itself with scientific ideas and with philosophical opinions which have entered ordinary life'.[12] Thus ideologies come to be seen as 'common sense' and practices are shaped accordingly. With regard to mothering and motherhood, as with regard to so much else, we have a patriarchal conceptualization.[13] The essence of what this means is, in Oakley's words, that we live in 'a culture which sets up people other than mothers as arbiters of "standards" of mothering work'.[14]

It is interesting that until relatively recently the majority of writing and research on aspects of mothering has been produced by men. However, they have seldom turned their attention on themselves as fathers, although, as Hearn points out, this is an historical change for in the eighteenth century childrearing manuals were addressed to fathers.[15] This has been the case with regard to obstetric practice and preparation for childbirth,[16] psychological research,[17] and popular 'how to' child care manuals.[18] Practically all of this work has been based on observation, sometimes in decontextualized laboratory situations. While this meets the demands of positivist science it does not explore the reality of the experiences it claims to be concerned with. Women's feelings and experiences as mothers have rarely been researched, 'the variety of situations in which women mother are generally not considered . . . knowledge about motherhood tends, therefore, to be assumed rather than examined'.[19] The effect has been to create prescriptions against which real mothers will measure themselves, frequently fail, and will then experience considerable guilt. This guilt tends to be exacerbated because a fundamental assumption on which much of this work of mothering is based, is the assumption of the 'natural' mother.[20]

'NATURAL' MOTHERING?

This assumption is insidious and pervasive. In spite of my belief, based on the reading and research I have done in the course of this work, that 'mothering' is socially constructed, every time I interviewed a mother teacher I ended up feeling inept and not such a 'proper' or 'natural' mother to my children, as they were to theirs. I even felt this with women who were much newer to the job than I was. It didn't matter that, at the same time, most of them were telling me of their anxieties about how they were doing, I still felt guilty. It may be, of course, that our concerns are not misplaced and that we constitute an aberrant group, but somehow I doubt it. Much more plausible is the argument that 'instinct', 'natural' and 'normal' are all concepts that are brought to bear to regulate and control women. Cosslett[21] shows how even the notion of 'natural' childbirth is not what it seems and yet the ideology has gained such a hold that women often feel failures if they confess to being in pain during labour. In a study of experiences of childbirth Ann Oakley found that women, indoctrinated with this ideology, felt that 'they were misled into thinking childbirth is a piece of cake and motherhood a bed of roses'.[22] Women said such things to her as

> You're not allowed to call them pains, are you? They're contractions. It always makes me laugh when I read that because I *knew* they bloody well hurt;[23] I felt I'd been *tricked,* actually *tricked,* by the health visitor, by the books I'd read – by the Gordon Bourne book, because he said the word 'pain' should *not* be applied to labour contractions.[24]

Having been there, even though my labours were quick and easy, 'natural', four-hour affairs, I can confirm that contractions hurt like hell and semantic sleight-of-hand does nothing to diminish that fact! Having said that, I have to acknowledge that I have been influenced by the ideology to the extent of feeling 'proud' of the speed at which I delivered even though I personally did nothing active to achieve this. I was 'lucky'; others are not as fortunate.

There is something of a paradox here because taking the line that childbirth is a 'natural' female process can be read and understood as an assertion of women's power and autonomy. Feminists have been eager to take back control of birth from the mainly male obstetricians who, in Western society, have come to dominate the scene. This again can be interpreted as slotting women into 'natural', gender-specific roles and thereby reinforcing the existing order.

Of course, it doesn't stop with the production of a child. The discourse that emphasises 'naturalness' and which also has the support of science influences thinking and 'common sense' concerning what are seen as essential aspects of child care and mothering. Harlow's work on 'bonding', for example, together with Bowlby's research into 'maternal deprivation' have played a significant part in making women feel bad if they don't immediately fall madly in love with their babies and guilty if they need to leave them in order to work. Some of the teachers I talked with had been caught by this 'trap'. They experienced something of a difficult moral dilemma with regard to going to work with other people's children while someone else looked after their child. On the one hand they did not agree with what they were doing, indeed their professional training had taught many of them that by working they would damage their child; but on the other hand, for various reasons, they needed to work.

Although Bowlby and Harlow both made considerable claims for what constitutes 'natural' mothering, the 'validity' and 'reliability' they purport to have for their work are now recognized as being highly questionable because these were decontextualized experiments, one with monkeys in a laboratory, the other with boys who were already in prison. And yet, because their findings supported the dominant ideology, buttressed by particular economic circumstances, that mothers should look after their children in the home, these methodological problems were ignored and they achieved wide currency:

> psychology, particularly developmental psychology, has provided support for ideas on motherhood that are helped by many politicians, paediatricians, obstetricians and popular writers. It has done so because many psychologists keep their own experiences isolated from their research in the name of scientific objectivity. Yet although they consider themselves to be using objective measures, they take 'commonsense' ideas about motherhood for granted without recognizing that these have specific ideological underpinnings.[25]

What this means is that the specificity with regard to culture, to social class and ethnicity that is bound up in these 'ideological underpinnings' also fails to be acknowledged. The models of childbirth and rearing which are so frequently held up as the 'norm' and the 'ideal' are, almost exclusively, based on middle-class, Anglo-Saxon, heterosexual definitions.[26] Even feminist writers have failed to contextualize their theories of motherhood and have, thereby, excluded so many mothers[27] and, at the same time, made another major contribution to maternal guilt.

So, according to the dominant ideology, what is this 'natural', 'normal', ideal mother like?

'Normal', 'natural' mothers love their babies as soon as, or even before, they are born.[28] The terms in which this early love is described can be directly traced to Harlow's experiments with baby monkeys on the basis of which he proposed the hypothesis of 'bonding'. However, this simian link is not always acknowledged. A widely read, popular, British magazine for pregnant women and new mothers emphasised the importance of the process:

> Mums have always fallen in love with their babies but until recently, we didn't have a name for these strong emotions. Today though, we talk about 'bonding' . . . babies deprived of this attachment fail to thrive physically as well as emotionally. Also, by forming a powerful relationship with you, your baby is laying down the foundations for his future relationships in life. And what's more, bonding is one of the most satisfying experiences life can offer.[29]

Paula Yates (a British celebrity) put even more emphasis on the naturalness of bonding when she wrote about it in her *Practical Guide to the Bliss of Babies*:

> Bonding should start the second your baby is born, and is the process by which the two of you fall in love. It is your time to woo your new baby into

loving you, and the beginning of your love for her. It is nature's way of ensuring that babies survive: babies are genetically programmed to attract their mothers so that their needs are met. . . . Bonding isn't hard work, it's falling head over heels in love with a little bit of heaven on your doorstep, dressed in a pink or blue babygrow.[30]

This does happen. Lesley, whose distress at her pregnancy was quoted earlier, experienced it:

I was going to take the full maternity leave and then go back and get a child-minder. Anyone would do I thought. And then she was born. The first day I was just sort of shellshocked. I'd had a very, very difficult labour, very painful indeed for the first one, and then I just got to picking her up on the second day, after I'd had a long sleep and, I don't know, I fell in love with her. And I said to G that night, 'I don't want to go back to work.' (*Lesley*)

Along with, or instead of the love, mothers mentioned a terrifying sense of responsibility:

Being a full-time mum means being the main carer for your child during the twenty-four hours of the day and the seven days of the week. You're where the buck stops. Other people may be doing it at other times but, at the end of the day, it's down to you and that is what I felt when she was, say, a couple of weeks old and it suddenly dawned on me. At first it was an awful realization but after a while I thought, this is great! I like being the one that's in control. I like being the one that's in charge and I don't have to answer to anybody else. . . . It's like being a teacher only more so, without somebody watching over you, the head or whatever, and that's a big attraction. (*Helen*)

I remember thinking when I was pregnant, 'My God! What have I done?' Yes, you do, because you're responsible, and I still go in to him at night, and with Sarah, you know, *my* babies. You're responsible for this new life. (*Gillian*)

This feeling is not limited to mothers, for James also experienced it, although perhaps not in quite the same way:

Being a parent means being totally responsible for somebody that's, well, not yours, but you've brought them into the world. (*James*)

Having fallen in love and become aware of their responsibilities 'natural', or as my mum would say, 'normal' mothers also fall into voluntary, unconditional and selfless thrall to their child. This means that they alway put their own needs and desires second. To paraphrase the words of the mothers quoted at the start of the chapter, they put their lives on hold and sacrifice themselves for their children. They do this because, in the end, what the child needs, the mother needs also. Penelope Leach, author of a best-selling British baby- and child-care book unequivocally, though somewhat casuistically, spells this out, although, unusually, she does also address the father in her advice on parenting:

> taking the baby's point of view does not mean neglecting yours, the parents', viewpoint. Your interests and his are identical. You are all on the same side; the side that wants to be happy, to have fun. If you make happiness for him he will make happiness for you. If he is unhappy, you will find yourself unhappy as well, however much you want or intend to keep your feelings separate from his.[31]

What this can come to mean is that,

> the ideal mother has no interests of her own. . . . For all of us it remains self-evident that the interests of mother and child are identical, and it is the generally acknowledged measure of the goodness or badness of the mother how far she really feels this identity of interest.[32]

This identity of interest demands that mothers become super-sensitive to their babies' needs. Mothers have to know, without being told, what their children require if they are to thrive and prosper. They must be constantly vigilant if they are to do this properly, hence the lack of room and time for themselves. How are they to know what is necessary? The assumption is that, with the help of instinct, mothers learn to recognize the signs that relate to what are believed to be objective needs. Christine Everingham, however, questions this assumption and suggests that what is really going on when a mother responds to a child's actions is that she is making a judgemental interpretation, influenced by the context of the 'mothering culture' to which she subscribes and/or belongs.[33]

'NATURAL', 'GOOD' MOTHERS AS TEACHERS

As well as being sensitive, mothers are required to be creative, especially in constructing learning situations for their children to experience. Thus doing the housework and baking cakes in such a way that these jobs become vehicles for communication skills, reading and arithmetic, and redesignating or adapting everyday implements so that they become toys, are all essential if the child is to have a 'good start' in life.[34] What is conveniently forgotten by this rhetoric is that not every mother has the resources, the inclination or the aptitude to do what is required. But if they don't do it they may be seen as 'bad' mothers, and they put their children at risk. As a result of their training, teacher mothers are, perhaps, especially aware of what they *should* be doing:

> I used to sit there when I was breast feeding. I really wanted to read a book but I knew I ought to be talking to him. So there I'd be chatting away about all sorts of crap. What we were going to do, what the prime minister was going to do, why it rained, you name it, and I really wanted to read a book. And I don't know if it made any difference. I doubt it somehow. (*Jenny*)

> The trouble was, having read Piaget and all the rest, and read child development books, you had this sort of feeling you had to do the right thing and I can remember getting to lunch time and thinking, God! I haven't said anything to that child for three hours. You know? Because she'd be happy playing and I'd be doing something else and we hadn't spoken. And I remember thinking it's a wonder this child's oral development isn't arrested. So I think, actually, a little bit of knowledge created an anxiety that needn't have been there. If I hadn't read the books and not known what I should've been doing I'd have gone on doing what naturally felt right for both of us; I don't suppose it made any difference to her, but it certainly would have stopped me getting quite so anxious about my status as a mother and my inadequacy. (*Rebecca*)

> Being with the same children all day (which is why I'm going back to work when my maternity leave is finished) would drive me batty. And doing the things they want to do, I mean I do it with Robert really. You know, I'd rather read the paper sometimes, than play with him and I know that's terrible and, to be honest, I do do that and I say, 'Look, go and play', and I just couldn't stand them round me all the time. (*Gillian*)

> When I was bringing my children up I remember one of the things that stuck in my mind from college, one of the things I encountered there was in the very first week. They were talking about the nature nurture debate that was very prevalent at the time. And one tutor gave an example of a mother who'd had this child and she wanted the child to grow up and be very intelligent and so she spent all her waking hours entertaining the child from it being a baby. And she'd do all her housework when the child slept and the child turned out to be brilliant. This was the story. She read to it, she'd play games, she'd sing to it, she'd just show it things and all this. So I remember thinking at the age of 18, right, when I have a child, I'll do that. And it

stuck with me for some reason. And to a large extent I tried to do that with L and although I was knackered, I succeeded. I tried it to a lesser extent with S and succeeded to a lesser extent because I was even more knackered. So what it meant was the way I interacted with her as a child, as a baby and as a toddler, was in a kind of teacher role. I'd take her for a walk in the pushchair. She couldn't speak, she was that young, she couldn't talk, she was four, five months old, and I saw other mothers taking their babies in push chairs and they'd cover ten times as much ground as I would in the time available. So I'd walk say, about ten yards, it'd take me about five or ten minutes because I'd be saying, 'Here's a wall. Let's feel the wall', and I'd get her hand, 'Touch the wall. Is it rough? It's rough. This is rough. Look at the trees. Look how tall they are. Tall.' You know? Oh God! I mean it's bloody exhausting and bloody boring. But I did this. I sustained this as far as I was able. I don't know whether it worked or not. I've been to school this morning to see her teacher and (she's extremely advanced in her English). I don't know whether that had anything to do with it or not. We'll never know. Who the hell knows? But that's what I was trying to do. . . . I would not allow her to sit there, doing nothing, except for the odd minute. I'd be talking to her and the effort would be sheer, bloody boring. I hated it but I would do it. I'd throw a ball up in the air and say 'Up it goes. Down it comes.' (*Lesley*)

Such responsibility is exhausting, especially, perhaps, if the mother does the 'right thing', and stays at home to look after her children. It is, however, supposed to bring what is regarded as the ultimate reward, that is utter fulfilment,[35] for

you are going to know this person better than you will ever know anybody else. Nobody else in the world including your partner, however devoted, is ever going to love you as much as your baby will in these first years if you will let him. You are into a relationship which is unique and which can therefore be uniquely rewarding.[36]

For some people, however, the gratification seems to be deferred:

Being a mum is hard work. I think it's harder work being a mum than going out to work. Definitely, without a shadow of a doubt. . . . It's hard work and I don't think you get the reward straight away, with being a mum. I think it's drudgery. (*Gillian*)

In addition to the demands of society and the ideology, each baby itself seems to want a particular kind of mother.[37] This was certainly the case with my two and everyone else seems to say the same. Thus there are demands all round and these can come to seem overwhelming.

> When I was pregnant I thought it would be the thing that would make me joyously happy for evermore. And it doesn't. No, it certainly doesn't. Sometimes, certainly since I had Sarah, this is a dreadful thing to say, but I remember phoning my mum up and saying, 'Look, I just can't. Just come and take them away. I just don't want them any-more. I want to go back to being what I was before.' But I didn't mean it. Well, I did, but not permanently. I think you need help. All this business about doing it on your own is just rubbish. (*Gillian*)

CHANGING IDEOLOGIES OF MOTHERHOOD

The nature of the demands does, however, change as social contexts change. Gillian, for example, refers to the isolation experienced by many mothers in these days when small family units, sometimes as small as a mother and a child, are not uncommon. As was noted earlier, dominant ideologies are contested, adapted, altered or replaced but always the ideologies that remain reflect the contemporary zeitgeist and the requirements of those in a position to influence thinking. With regard to motherhood, an examination of dominant thinking at different historical times reveals that mothers have been expected to be increas-ingly active in the socialization and pre-school education of their children. Being given more responsibility means that there is more room for 'failure', it also means that more demands are made on mothers to actively 'mother'.

For example: about ten years ago my next-door neighbour had a baby and went back to work leaving the child in the care of her mother-in-law. Every morning, regardless of the weather, from October through to March, the baby would be put outside in a large, robust carriage pram. There she would remain for most of the day, being taken inside for feeds and to be changed. Despite my lack of interest in babies at that time, I did begin to feel concerned, largely, I expect, as a result of what I had learnt during my teacher training. Even I knew that babies *needed* constant stimulation while they were awake; surely being left in this way was not a good thing. I also wondered if the baby was in any dan-ger from the cold. I wasn't the only one who was perturbed. Someone actually reported what was going on to a local health visitor. When she went round to check up, the grandmother was extremely upset. She was only doing what she had been told to do with her own babies, forty years previously: she even had the books that told her. I too have a 1957 edition of a book first published in 1944, which takes the same line. Thus,

> It is a mistake to think that a tiny baby must be wheeled out in his pram every day. If you have to go out shopping and cannot leave him asleep in the garden with someone within hearing, then it cannot be helped. But ideally

baby should sleep out of doors all day, winter or summer, and the less he is wheeled about the better, until he is old enough to sit up and take notice, which is not usually until six or seven months. The only weather which is really unsuitable for baby is fog. Rain will not harm him at all, if the storm-cover on his pram and hood are up. On cold days put him in his warm pram-suits with feet attached to them, and gloves, too, if possible. If he chews his gloves until they are sodden and cold, make a pair of loose wash-leather bags to cover the woollen ones, and attach them to the sleeves. A bonnet should not be necessary until he is sitting up. Baby can be put out within a few days of his birth.[38]

Compare this with Penelope Leach's advice on 'Keeping your baby warm':

a short trip in his pram with the air temperature in the 50s will not hurt him . . . a whole morning in the pram in the garden is a different matter. Why should he be forced to work at keeping warm for so long when he could get just as much fresh air beside an open window?[39]

By putting her baby outside, the 1950s mother did not only believe that she was doing the child good, she also had much more time to do her own work, which, at that time, would have been expected to be housework. Admittedly this would have been much more onerous in those days, without the aid of such things as automatic washing machines, disposable nappies, powerful vacuum cleaners, wonder detergents, microwave cookers and one-stop supermarkets, but she still had the time. If the baby cried she was told that it was 'exercising' its lungs and, given time to learn that crying didn't produce anything, the baby would give up. So, the husband and father could return to a clean home, his dinner on the table, and as likely as not, the baby already in bed. Mothers who did not manage this were regarded as 'bad' wives. Nowadays, as well as keeping house and probably going out to work, mothers are expected to stimulate their babies, as we have already seen. Penelope Leach's book, for example, contains five pages devoted to 'playing and learning' during the first six months, in addition to four pages on strategies for encouraging hand–eye co-ordination. By comparison, the *Good Housekeeping* book that was first written in the 1940s, does not advise any play at all until the end of the first year.

Then there is feeding on demand. Whether feeding by breast or, much less satisfactorily according to the ideology, by bottle, mothers these days are recommended to feed on demand rather than, as their grandmothers were, to a timetable. While this does tend to mean that babies cry less and are more content it does further erode the mother's time for herself and controls her behaviour even more.

Once again, it is difficult to know what is ideology and what is really in the best interests of the child. For instance I believe that cuddling and kissing are good for babies and children (and adults for that matter); it seems 'common sense' to me but it is also part of the present-day orthodoxy of ideal motherhood, so I cannot know for certain where my belief originates. A couple of generations ago mothers were told that such behaviour spoilt, and was bad for, children and they thought that this was 'common sense' too. Maybe the truth of the matter is that we just don't know what is best practice. If instinct and 'nature' were all there is to it mothers would not have to be told what to do: but it is not that simple. Babies and mothers are all different and have different idiosyncratic needs that sometimes are met and sometimes are not. Blanket prescriptions are just inappropriate but then if ideologies are there to support social orders, the needs of individuals are, in any case, irrelevant.

And in spite of the specific changes in ideology, including changes in what is considered acceptable and appropriate for women, women still remain the primary child carers[40] both in the home and in nurseries and schools. There has been little or no deviation from this way of organizing things. Although modern or 'New' men are often said to have more to do with their children, there is little 'objective' evidence that actually supports the idea that this is happening in any sense of large numbers of men taking an equal share in child care.[41] However, the majority of the women I spoke with said that their partners did take a far more active role with their children than their own fathers had and the men I talked with all spoke of their practical involvement in child care. This could have been: because they were teachers; because, practically, they had more time and opportunity to be involved; because they had more experience of children; because their work had made them more aware than many other men of the importance of parental input; and because they were less concerned to meet stereotypical expectations. One man, James, had actually been the primary carer for his child while his wife worked full time:

> When L was pregnant with Ruby she got the chance of a job in an FE college and we decided that she should take this and go straight back to work while I looked after the baby. In the end I went part time and the baby went to a minder and then a nursery part time. It seemed the best solution to us because I wanted to look after her and I enjoy that sort of thing much more than L, and L's job prospects were better than mine, her new job was at a more senior level than me so it made sense to do it like that and it's worked out really well. (*James*)

Karen's husband had also left work in order to look after their children while she pursued her career.

Looking through a poetry anthology recently, I came across a poem by Hugh McDiarmid entitled 'The Two Parents'. In this the poet describes the different responses of a mother and a father to their son's illness; the mother stays by the bedside whilst the father felt confined and impatient. The poem ends by suggesting that, faced with a similar situation, all women behave in the same way and implies that this is a fundamental difference between the sexes. While it is still the case that women tend to do most of the caring for sick children, it is questionable whether they have a greater 'natural' aptitude for this work. James would not accept that they have, nor would Brian, Dennis or Stuart:

> My wife was actually a children's nurse before we got married but I've always been the one who looks after the kids when they're ill. She hasn't got the patience. I think she wants it to be more like a hospital ward, and it's also that she gets upset when it's ours. Not that they've really been ill much, thank God. (*Brian*)

> Obviously we got very acquainted, too acquainted, with nursing during S's illness. We were with him all the time, and so was [his sister]. As it became clearer that he wasn't going to get better we did more and more. It was very difficult at times but we did everything for him. (*Dennis*)

> My wife is hopeless when the kids are ill. She gets very anxious and irritable because she's worried. I cope with my worries by doing things. She'll tell you, I'm the better nurse. (*Stuart*)

We have come a long way since 1948 when a magazine could get away with an article on fathers' responsibilities that said

> Am I hinting that Father should wash the nappies and the crockery whenever he has time to spare? I am not! I think he has done his bit. And a heavy bit it is apt to be – when he has shouldered the role of breadwinner. The children should admire him for it, and Mother should teach them how. . . . Before the child has been long in this world, at his first moment of consecutive observation, he is aware that the ruler of his life is Father. Between him and Father, of course, is a softer creature – but depending on Father, on his moods and his incalculable valuations.[42]

WOMAN = MOTHER?

Even those politicians and right-wing commentators who, at the present time, are talking up the need to 'return' to 'traditional' family structures, would hesitate to put things quite so bluntly as the article quoted above (although they would probably agree with the sentiments that are expressed). But even without such blatancy the dominant ideology still works to keep the women with the children and out of the other forums which men want for themselves. And it will continue to do this as long as the notion that real women are essentially mothers retains its commonsense status. Comments such as the following by Sheila Kitzinger deny that not all women want to be mothers: 'A woman expresses herself in childbearing. Without this experience she feels she has missed something, that she is incomplete, in some way, wasted.'[43] As well as restricting and subordinating women, this belief can cause considerable suffering to women who are unable, for various reasons, to bear the children that they wish for. It damaged my mother, hurt me, and devastated Nicola:

> I had my suspicions that it (conception) might be difficult . . . and subsequent investigations revealed that, because of my previous medical history it was going to be well nigh impossible. It took five years to get to that stage due to the incompetencies of various doctors and by the time we were beginning to realize that and starting on an IVF programme at Barts, we decided to put our names down for adoption. . . . It took nine years from the date of our marriage to our getting our daughter (through adoption). . . . Before I had her I used to hate babies: not hate them, I was antagonistic to their mothers. If I heard my sister-in-law, or even worse, my sister, was pregnant, that was it. In the end it got so bad I wouldn't even go to parties if I knew someone was coming with a new baby. I refused to go. My husband would say, 'Don't be so bloody stupid', and I'd say, 'I don't wish to see it flaunted in front of my face.' (*Nicola*)

I worry too that my own daughter's happiness and experience of her life may be adversely affected by this insidious notion. Aged 5 as I write this, Robyn is desperately fond of babies to the extent that seeing a friend's new-born for the first time the other day, she was so overcome that she could barely speak. She tells me that when she grows up she is going to have 'lots of babies, at least six, to love, even when they're naughty, and to look after. I'll buy them lots of toys and let them sit on my knee all day when they're poorly. I'll teach them to swim and dance with them and I'll always give them sweeties when they cry.' Of course, there is a long way to go yet and her views may very well change. But what if they don't and what if she can't have children? Will her life be ruined? And why does she feel like this? Steedman *et al* suggest that it is because 'women have been defined primarily in terms of their capacities for bearing and rearing children. This definition not only curtails their opportunities for finding an alternative language, but permeates their desires: women want to be what they have been made to be.'[44] The argument is that women are brought up to believe and to expect that they will become mothers and so, following this, I must bear some of the responsibility for Robyn's ambitions.

Taking a psychoanalytic approach, Nancy Chodorow offers a persuasive account of how the pattern of female mothering is reproduced. She argues that

> an investigation of the child's experience of being mothered shows that fundamental expectations of women as mothers emerge during this period. . . . The character of the infant's early relation to its mother profoundly affects its sense of self . . . and its feelings about its mother and women in general.[45]

For boys, however, the lesson is different: 'that women mother and men do not is projected back by the child after gender comes to count. Women's early mothering, then, creates specific conscious and unconscious attitudes or expectations in women.'[46] These are further reinforced by what children see around them in society.

Of course, it doesn't happen quite as smoothly as Chodorow's description suggests; hers is, after all only a theoretical model. Other factors of various kinds may intervene to make women want other things from their lives than children. Also, given that personal experiences of mothering are central, it follows that certain experiences may teach that being a mother is not desirable. Carolyn Steedman, for example, writes of how she, and other women, learnt from their mothers that children 'ruin your life' and are a nuisance.[47] She argues that the psychoanalytic approach excludes many women, often, but not exclusively, from the 'working classes', and stresses that, 'accounts of mothering need to recognize not-mothering, and recognizing it, would have to deal in economic circumstances and the social understanding that arises out of such circumstances'.[48] Such recognition and contextualization would seem to be essential in any case, if different experiences are to be acknowledged.

It is an appalling shame that women's lives are circumscribed by ideologies of motherhood but, in my view, it is also sad when alternative, feminist, ideologies denigrate the positive experiences many women obtain from being mothers. The notion of 'false consciousness' when applied in this context seems to be patronizing in the extreme. What is necessary is to listen to individual mothers talking about motherhood because what is then heard is often 'something that is very different from enshrined sociological typifications of this condition',[49] even though it is often couched in the vocabulary of dominant discourses. Lacking an alternative language there is little else that can honestly be done.

Returning to my daughter I should perhaps add that she does not see her future entirely in terms of motherhood. She asked me the other day whether I thought she would be able to spend more time with her children if she was a hospital doctor or if she was a 'doctor doctor', i.e. a GP. Such questions give me some confidence to think that she will have her cake and eat it too! But then she is, of course, in many respects, a relatively privileged girl. Others are nowhere near as lucky.

NOTES

1   Bennett, A., *Writing Home,* London, Faber & Faber, 1994.
2   Kristeva, J., 'Stabat Mater' in Toril Moi (ed.), *The Kristeva Reader,* Oxford, Basil Blackwell, 1986, pp. 178–9.
3   Cosslett, T., *Women Writing Childbirth: Modern Discourses of Motherhood,* Manchester, Manchester University Press, 1994, p. 117.
4   Gieves, K., 'Introduction' in Gieves, K. (ed.) *Balancing Acts: On Being a Mother,* London, Virago, 1989, p. viii.
5   Cosslett, *op. cit.,* p. 19.

6   Gimenez, M., 'Feminism, Pronatalism and Motherhood' in Treblicott, J. (ed.), *Mothering: Essays in Feminist Theory,* Maryland, Rowman and Littlefield, 1983, p. 287.

7   See, for instance, Badinter, E., *The Myth of Motherhood,* trans. by R. DeGaris, London, Souvenir Press, 1981; de Beauvoir, S., *The Second Sex,* trans. and ed. H. Parshley, London, Cape, 1953; contributors to Glenn, E., Chang, G. and Forcey, L. (eds), *Mothering: Ideology, Experience and Agency,* New York, Routledge, 1994; Rich, A., *Of Woman Born: Motherhood as Experience and Institution,* London, 1986; Steedman, C., Urwin, C. and Walkerdine, V. (eds), *Language, Gender and Childhood,* London, Routledge & Kegan Paul, 1985; contributors to Treblicot, J. (ed.), *Mothering: Essays in Feminist Theory,* Maryland, Rowman & Littlefield, 1983.

8   Firestone, S., *The Dialectic of Sex,* London, Cape, 1970.

9   For example, Andrews, J., *In Praise of the Anecdotal Woman: Motherhood and a Hidden Curriculum,* Stoke-on-Trent, Trentham Books, 1994; Cosslett, *op. cit.*; Everingham, C., *Motherhood and Modernity,* Buckingham, Open University Press, 1994; Gieves, *op. cit.*; contributors to Glenn et al, 1994; Grumet, M., *Bitter Milk: Women and Teaching,* Amherst, University of Massachusetts, 1988; Ruddick, S., 'Maternal Thinking', in Treblicott, J. (ed.) *Mothering: Essays in Feminist Theory,* Maryland, Rowman & Littlefield, 1983.

10   Glenn et al, *op. cit.*

11   Ibid, pp. 22–3.

12   Gramsci, A., *Selections From the Prison Notebooks* (eds Q. Hoare and Nowell-Smith), London, Lawrence & Wishart, 1971, p. 326n.

13   Andrews, *op. cit.*; Everingham, *op. cit.*; Glenn et al, *op. cit.*

14   Oakley, A., *Social Support and Motherhood,* Oxford, Basil Blackwell, 1992, p. 188.

15   Hearn, J., *Men In the Public Eye,* London, Routledge, 1992, p. 109.

16   For example, Michel Odent, Grantly Dick Read, Frederick Leboyer, Fernand Lamaze.

17   For example, James Bowlby, Harry Harlow, Derek Winnicott.

18   For example, Benjamin Spock, Hugh Jolly.

19   Phoenix, A., Woolett, A. and Lloyd, E. (eds), *Motherhood: Meanings, Practices and Ideologies,* London, Sage, 1991, p. 2.

20   Rich, *op. cit.*, pp. 22–3.

21   Cosslett, *op. cit.*

22   Oakley, A., 'Interviewing Women – A Contradiction in Terms' in Roberts, H. (ed.), *Doing Feminist Research,* London, Routledge, 1981, p. 6.

23   Ibid, p. 87.

24   Ibid, p. 109.

25   Phoenix et al, *op. cit.*, p. 20.

26   See Hill Collins, P., 'Shifting the Centre: Race, Class and Feminist Theorizing About Motherhood', in Glenn, E., Chang, G. and Forcey, L. (eds), *Mothering: Ideology, Experience and Agency,* New York, Routledge, 1994; Lewin, E., 'Negotiating Lesbian Motherhood: The Dialectics of Resistance and Accommodation'. in Glenn, E., Chang, G. and Forcey, L. (eds), *Mothering: Ideology, Experience and Agency,* New York, Routledge, 1994; Walkerdine, V. and Lucey, H., *Democracy in the Kitchen: Regulating Mothers and Socialising Daughters,* London, Virago, 1989.

27   Spelman, E., *Inessential Woman: Problems of Exclusion in Feminist Thought,* Boston, Beacon Press, 1988.

28   Walkerdine and Lucey, *op. cit.*, p. 60.

29   *Mother & Baby,* 'True Love: That Magical Bond With Your Baby', August 1994, p.8.

30   Yates, P., *The Fun Starts Here: A Practical Guide to the Bliss of Babies,* London, Bloomsbury, 1990, pp. 110–11.

31   Leach, P., *Baby and Child: From Birth to Age Five,* London, Penguin, 1989, p. 8.

32   Balint, A., 'Love For the Mother and Mother Love' in Balint, A. (ed.), *Primary Love and Psychoanalytic Technique,* New York, Liveright Publishing Company, 1939.

33   Everingham, *op. cit.*

34   See Walkerdine and Lucey, *op. cit.*; Leach, *op. cit.*

35   Urwin, C., 'Constructing Motherhood: The Persuasion of Normal Development' in Steedman, C., Urwin, C. and Walkerdine, V. (eds), *Language, Gender and Childhood,* London, Routledge & Kegan Paul, 1985, p. 118.

36   Leach, *op. cit.*, p. 13.

37   Gieves, *op. cit.*, p. 44.

38   Good Housekeeping, *Good Housekeeping's Baby Book,* London, National Magazine Company Ltd, 1957, pp. 104–105.

39   Leach, *op. cit.*, p. 81.

40   See McKee, L. and O'Brien, M. (eds), *The Father Figure,* London, Tavistock, 1982; Lewis, C. and O'Brien, M. (eds), *Reassessing Fatherhood: New Observations on Fathers and the Modern Family,* London, Sage, 1987.

41   Morgan, D., *Discovering Men,* London, Routledge, 1992; Ve, H., 'The Male Gender Role and Responsibility for Children', in Boh, K. et al (eds), *Changing Patterns of European Family Life,* London, Routledge, 1989.

42   Edginton, M., 'No Greater Kingdom', *Mother and Home,* November 1948, pp. 44–5.

43   Kitzinger, S., *The Experience of Childbirth,* 5th edn., Harmondsworth, Penguin, 1984, p. 68.

44   Steedman, C., Urwin, C. and Walkerdine, V. (eds), *Language, Gender and Childhood,* London, Routledge & Kegan Paul, 1985, p. 3.

45   Chodorow, N., *The Reproduction of Mothering: Psychoanalysis and the Sociology of Gender,* Berkeley, University of California Press, 1978, p. 77.

46   Ibid, p. 83.

47   Steedman, C., *The Tidy House,* London, Virago, 1982; Steedman, C., *Landscape For A Good Woman: A Story of Two Lives,* London, Virago, 1986.

48   Steedman, *op. cit.*, p. 88.

49   Oakley, *op. cit.*, p. 343.

Chapter 4

'In Loco Parentis'
Teacher as Parent

INTRODUCTION

> Sometimes they get mixed up and they call you 'mum'. When they get a bit older some of them are terribly embarrassed when they realize what they've said, but that's what you are for them, while they're in school. You are there as a sort of surrogate parent. I've got a male friend who's head of an infant school and they call him mum too, not dad, I don't know whether it means anything but it seems significant, they expect him to be a mum, to be a woman. (*Margaret*)

> They need security, even from a teacher, especially from a teacher, because you are a replacement parent at that time. To a certain extent you are *in loco parentis*, but very warily because some parents would take umbrage at it. But having said that, if I've got kids in the classroom then I want a relationship with them that they can trust me. (*Katie*)

Traditionally, and in law, teachers have been considered to be *in loco parentis* with regard to their students. When corporal punishment was legal in state schools, teachers were expected to discipline, and, if they deemed it necessary, to hit children in line with what a 'responsible' and 'reasonable' parent would do. Such expectations are based on commonsense notions of parental behaviours, attitudes, beliefs and values. These notions involve sex role stereotypes for mothers and fathers, some of which were explored in the previous chapter. Consequently teaching has come to be constructed and shaped as a gendered profession based on familial roles[1] and ideas about ideal mothers and fathers have been conflated with ideas about ideal female and male teachers. This has implications for dominant ideologies of teaching, the ensuing practice of teachers, and for teachers' career experiences. In this chapter I want to consider some of these implications and to look at how teachers experience them. The focus will be on women teachers' perceptions and experiences because, in schools as in society generally, when it comes to the family, it is the role of the mother, rather than that of the father, which is prominent and which is emphasised as being of greatest significance to the emotional, intellectual and physical development of the child.

MOTHERS IN TEACHING

In Britain (and in other Western nations) the majority of teachers, in secondary as well as in primary schools, are women. Fundamentally, the reasons for this are to do with the taken-for-granted assumption, and the reality, that women, i.e. mothers, look after children. Thus, working with children is advocated as an appropriately feminine thing to do: school hours appear to fit in conveniently with a woman's commitment to her own children and to her husband; and teaching offers a relatively 'good' salary for a woman. Traditionally, teaching has also provided an opportunity for working-class people to get a higher education and, by implication, to move up the social class ladder (which was the case for me and for a number of the informants). Consequently these reasons led to teaching often being recommended, by teachers and parents, as a 'good job for a girl'.

For many of the women I talked with, as for Kathleen Casey's teachers, the decision to teach was very much a pragmatic one, rather than being the fulfilment of a lifelong ambition.[2] This was especially true among the mature women entrants to teaching for whom the need to find a job which was compatible with child- and home-care was paramount. Liz's comments are typical of what they all said:

> When my eldest went into reception that was when I actually met someone who was training to be a teacher, who was also a mum with a child in that class, and I talked to her about it and realized it was possible to actually do it, because I didn't think I could until they were both 9 or 10, that sort of age. . . . I didn't think I could fit the training in around the children . . . but seeing this other person who I knew, who was actually divorced with three children, could do it, I thought, well, maybe I can after all. . . . I am very limited in what I can do, because of the family. Teaching is convenient, if it had caused much upheaval in the family I wouldn't have done it. (*Liz*)

For single parents the issue of work-home compatibility can be crucial:

> There's no way I'd teach if I didn't have Chris. No, I don't think I would. I think I'd finish the course and I'd do something else. There are a lot of things that I want to do and I know that I'm going to do them but I'm going to have to teach first just to get some money and become a bit more financially independent, and it also fits in with Chris, while he's at nursery and then infant school but I'm not going to teach for ever. (*Teresa*)

> After eight years teaching in primary school I left to have Richard. I left because I wanted to be at home for Richard. That's a very old-

fashioned view, isn't it? And I thought now I'm going to give my time to this baby. But that's when it all went wrong because that's when my husband left me. And I'd no job, I'd got this baby, had no home, and I'd lost all the security I had. My mother had just died, she died when Richard was six months old, and my dad was 74 and it was just chaotic. So really I then had to start and look for work which was what I didn't want to do, but I didn't have any choice. I was very lucky. I went back into nursery when Richard was about 3. He was eighteen months when my husband left. It took me two years to sort out the legal side of it. Then I went back into nursery and I just took him with me, so I was very, very lucky, and he had a full nursery day. . . . It was a big nursery so I could move him away from me, 'Richard, go and play somewhere else'. . . . I was there a few months so he came with me all the time and then he went to his own nursery. And the head at that school actually kept his place open for him because I did little bits of supply here and there, and she said, 'If you want to take Richard with you, you can. Fair enough, I'll leave his place open.' People were great really. So he used to do a couple of months at one nursery, go back to his own, couple of months at somebody else's, go back to his own. So he had a very varied nursery education. And then when he went into school I got a temporary contract for two years and I worked in a hearing impaired unit. . . . I went into nursery because that was what came up but also because it fitted in at a time when I was totally desperate really, because I didn't think I could leave him with my dad. My dad was getting older. Richard had never been a sleeper so a couple of hours, half a day with my dad was enough, and I just felt he was too old for that responsibility. . . . It's how things happen. It's life. Everything went totally wrong. (*Jane*)

Even for mothers who have a partner, fitting teaching in with family life is not as straightforward as it might initially seem. Karen's situation was unusual because it was her husband who stayed at home with the children while she went out to work but she still experienced considerable strain:

It was horrendous. I look back on it and I think Ugh! Because it was. There was no extended maternity leave. I was back to work six weeks after I'd had her and it was just really hard going. Pete stayed at home, he was a complete novice; well, with your first child you're both complete novices really, but he was suddenly at home looking after this six-week-old baby and running the house and thinking, 'Oh my God! What's going on?' I was at work and we didn't have transport then so I was travelling on two buses there and back. She was born in September so I went back to work in October and yeah, I was knackered basically. (*Karen*)

63

It is interesting that none of the father teachers mentioned any difficulties of this kind, even those who considered themselves to take an equal share of child care. It seems that they relied on their wives to do the fitting in and dashing around, even when they were also working outside of the home. On the other hand, however, it does appear that the mother teachers took it for granted that it had to be them who bore this responsibility, together with the guilt that is often associated with being a working mother and, therefore, actually doing two jobs.[3]

> I taught languages in a secondary school for two and three-quarter years then I left and had three kids. I gradually went back to part-time evening school teaching and some private tuition so in total I was only away from it for six years. Then after eight years I went back in to gradually building up to part-time teaching and when my youngest one started, I was doing virtually a full-time timetable. I went in at 9.05 a.m. after dropping him off at the nursery school and finished at 3.25 p.m. I did that and it meant a great deal of dashing around. (*Janice*)

> Getting child care once they start school is actually more difficult than when you need it full time. I despair sometimes because I'm always looking at the clock, knowing that, come what may, I'm going to have to leave at a certain time to pick them up from school. I get stressed out from it sometimes. (*Margaret*)

> As a working mum. . . . I had guilt feelings that I couldn't always go and help or do things [at my own children's school] and yet I was lucky because I saw the kids in assemblies and things and I was lucky because they were in my school. (*Sylvia*)

MOTHER TEACHERS AND CAREER DEVELOPMENT

Listening to and hearing accounts like those above does call into question the extent to which teaching really is a convenient and compatible job for a mother. Evidence also indicates[4] that it is not an especially 'good' career either, in terms of offering opportunities for promotion, for women in general and mothers in particular. This was certainly the experience of many of the women I talked to and while Jane, quoted earlier, had an extremely understanding head teacher, this would seem to be the exception, rather than the rule. Although, twenty years ago, Sylvia's husband was very supportive of her career, her head teacher had reservations:

> When I was pregnant with Robert I decided that I didn't really want to give up because if you gave up teaching you lost your scale post, by

then I'd got a scale post. . . . My parents were both working as head
teachers in the same LEA that I was in, my husband was away in the
navy, so they weren't available to look after the children, but my par-
ents-in-law said that they would. Then, as the time came nearer
George decided to buy himself out and he actually looked after Robert
half of the time because he worked shifts and got a job where he could
do this, deliberately so, and his parents did the other time and I did
after school and holidays. . . . The head at my school really carpeted
me about it. Maternity leave was short then, they weren't twenty-
nine weeks, they were eighteen weeks, eleven weeks before and seven
weeks after, and I remember him saying to me, 'What on earth do
your parents think about this?' I said, 'I'm married now and I'm going
to do it. My parents are quite happy. They know that the child won't
be neglected.' 'Yes but the school might be, very much.' I said, 'No it
won't.' I mean, this poor kid. I used to take rounders teams. I used to
pick him up from Grandma's or she'd drop him round in the carry-cot
and we'd be at the rounders match. (*Sylvia*)

Karen also faced some questioning.

When I had Lucy [eighteen years ago] people didn't have maternity
leave and come back to work and I had people saying to me, 'Oh, are
you really sure?', this was other teachers, 'Do you think you're doing
the right thing?' and all this. So looking back on it now there was
quite a lot of 'anti' feeling about me taking maternity leave and coming straight back to work, whereas now it's not an issue. (*Karen*)

Although conditions for maternity leave and return to work are much
more generous than they were when Sylvia and Karen had their children,
head teachers holding similar attitudes are still around. Gillian's experience
was, that in her head teacher's view, motherhood and teaching were not
compatible:

It's seen as separate, in that they don't combine, certainly in secondary schools. Most of my friends have left that school because he
won't give part-time work. . . . He's all right as long as you go back full
time and as long as you don't create any problems. I went back full
time after having Robert. Then Robert had to go into hospital when he
was one and I had to have a week and a bit off work and on the surface he was very good, he made all the right noises, but I lost all my
money. I was a bit miffed about that. He'd say, 'Oh yes, you have as
much time off as you like' and then, when it came to it, he wasn't very
understanding. . . . He doesn't value, there's no way he would contem-
plate part-timers. Most of my friends who wanted part-time work and

asked him, they've gone from the school. He won't even do job shares.
. . . I'm told other heads aren't like this. (*Gillian*)

Unfortunately, some are. Bob Burgess writes of a head who did not believe that mother teachers with babies and small children should work full time. This man's view was that 'Anybody, man or woman, who puts their career before their family is rather a dangerous person to have around.'[5] Put like this the majority of people would probably have some sympathy with such a view but it is usually mothers, rather than fathers, who feel that they are penalized for even trying to have a career, regardless of how they prioritize it.

Head teachers are clearly powerful people; gatekeepers when it comes to career progress. These days, in England and Wales, following the 1988 Education Reform Act, school governors are equally or even more powerful. Governors' views about who is an appropriate person for a particular job are reflected in who they appoint and promote. While equal opportunities laws make it illegal to discriminate it is impossible to legislate against deeply held beliefs. A quick glance at the sex of head teachers within the majority of, if not all, LEAs will reveal that more men occupy these positions and this pattern is repeated with regard to all promotion posts, despite there being more women teachers overall. In fact it does seem that, proportionately, even fewer women are getting headships than they did in previous years. Reorganization, from single-sex to co-educational secondary schools and from separate infant and junior to all-through primaries has been detrimental to women.[6] Karen had observed what was happening:

> There is now a culture of the young macho male primary head coming through and I'm sure it's governors' appointments. And the thing that's happening in [—] as well, which I think has been detrimental to women getting on is that schools have been amalgamated. They used to be separate infant and junior schools. Apart from one now every one's an all-through primary school so that's cut the traditional opportunities that were there for women as heads of infant schools. (*Karen*)

THE GENDERED AND FAMILIAL CHARACTER OF TEACHING

As Caroline Benn notes, this discrepancy in who occupies which positions is related to the gendered and familial character attached to teaching and teachers and it is nothing new:

> Historically, there have always been two distinct teaching functions: the first an extension of mothering, and reserved for women; the second an extension of power and authority, reserved for men, who have guarded it

well. This division – while no longer explicit – is still implicit throughout the education system.[7]

So, men are expected to be the disciplinarian fathers who are in charge of things, while women are the nurturing mother carers. A significant consequence of this, which feminists have frequently remarked upon, is that, every day, children see their teachers re-enacting stereotypical roles. This, it is argued, is likely to lead to social reproduction because it confirms taken-for-granted assumptions about what it is 'natural' for men and women to do. Leading on from this, and from the notion of teachers being *in loco parentis*, is the commonly held opinion that, in these days of an increasing number of single-parent families headed by mothers, it is more important for young children to come across male teachers as role models because they are not believed to have sufficient contact with suitable men. A more liberal view is that all youngsters can benefit from seeing men in caring, nurturing roles because this will help to break the cycle of reproduction. And yet men do not seem to be that eager to work with young children. At the university where I work very few male students are enrolled on primary-teaching courses. And our student profile is not substantially different from that of any other institution.

Reporting in 1925 a Board of Education Committee claimed to have 'identified a feeling that for a man to spend his life teaching children of school age is to waste it in easy and not very valuable work, he would not do it if fit for anything else'.[8] Nowadays it is unlikely that such sentiments would be expressed so blatantly but primary teaching is still seen as women's work to the extent that men wishing to work with young children may even have their sexuality questioned. Yet it is not simply that teaching is seen as work suitable for women, it is also that the work is to be done in a specifically feminine, motherly way.

THE MOTHER-MADE-CONSCIOUS MODEL OF TEACHING

Historical accounts of the development of primary schooling show how, over the last 200 to 250 years, a discourse, premised on the ideal teacher as the 'mother made conscious' has come to dominate ideology and practice.[9] In England and Wales, at least, this discourse reached its apogee with the publication, in 1967, of the influential Plowden Report entitled *Children and Their Primary Schools*.[10] Plowden insisted that children should be tenderly cared for and that primary teachers should be parent-substitutes, or, more accurately, substitute mothers, for it was assumed (quite reasonably, given the statistics) that they would be women. And teachers saw themselves in this role. Where 'father teachers' appeared, they tended to do so as headmasters or 'as the psychologist waiting in the wings'[11] ready to pick up the pieces when things went wrong. The infant-school teacher who told Ron King that 'We're their mothers while they are in school'[12] echoed both the rhetoric and what was, for many, the reality.

The sort of mother Plowden exhorted teachers to be is the 'natural', sensitive, child-centred, selfless kind discussed in the previous chapter. Thus teachers and student teachers were to be warm and caring and capable of developing intimate dyadic relationships with each child in their class. This would allow them to provide individualized learning experiences appropriate for the stage of development the child had reached. It would also help them in their vital task of exercising what Foucault calls 'moral technology', that is, encouraging children to become self-motivating and self-regulating. Just as Leach *et al* advocate. What has happened is that notions about what constitutes a 'good' mother (i.e. a 'good' woman) and a 'good' primary-school teacher have intertwined, and 'fed' each other with the outcome being almost identical dominant ideologies of mothering and of teaching.

It must be noted however, that throughout the late 1970s and the 1980s, critics, particularly those from the political right, although there were also worried voices from the left, were increasingly voicing their concerns about the Plowdenesque approach. The main worry was that a focus on the perceived needs of the individual, together with an emphasis on an integrated approach to knowledge and skills, could lead to the neglect of the so-called basics: that is, reading, writing and arithmetic. Some argued that working-class children were particularly disadvantaged by such approaches because they lacked the 'cultural capital', i.e. the background experiences and the sort of parental support which would allow them to get the full benefit from them. In other words, because they did not have 'ideal' mothers at home, as middle-class children were assumed to have, they did not know what was expected of them. Consequently they had to fathom this out before they could get on with the academic learning and if they didn't, they were 'lost'. Adult illiteracy, poor levels of 'basic' knowledge, unemployment, economic recession, rising crime rates, and an increasing incidence of births to unmarried women have all been attributed, in varying degrees, to child-centredness at school and also in the home. The government attempted to tackle the 'education problem' through the introduction of the 1988 Education Reform Act[13] and in particular by the National Curriculum with its emphasis on discrete subjects, levels of attainment, and testing. Concomitantly changes were also made to the curriculum in teacher education. The main change was to substantially decrease the amount of time spent in studying theoretical issues, especially sociological, psychological, and philosophical issues, and to increase the time spent in school and in learning how to 'deliver' the National Curriculum. Some teachers expressed concern about this:

> This is what worries me about teacher training now. I don't feel
> there's going to be that theoretical base, that, at the time, you may not
> feel is particularly valuable, but you refer back to it. . . . I worry about
> the teachers of the future. (*Karen*)

You don't think much of it at the time but I think you need a bit of
experience and then you look back and you think, ah yes! So that was
what that was all about. And I think you need it. (*Jane*)

Some of these teachers, they've been straight from school to college then
back to school and they've led nice little secure middle-class lives and
they don't have a clue. If they don't get the input on the sociology on the
things about race and class and gender then they are never going to
really begin to think about what's going on. I dread to think what it'll be
like in a few years time when no one's doing it. I think we had too much
but I don't think there's anywhere near enough now. (*Ann*)

There is no doubt that these changes to a more didactic approach will eventually influence ideologies of teaching because what is required of teachers has,
in some respects, changed, with a shift in emphasis from the development of the
whole child to an emphasis on the child's performance in the various curriculum
areas. This can also be seen in terms of it involving a shift in emphasis, albeit
slight owing to the resistance of teachers and teacher educators, from the primary teacher as mother, to the primary teacher as teacher. (Other countries
have also experienced similar shifts in thinking as the international zeitgeist
has changed.) In addition, governmental concern about the state of the social
order, which has been largely blamed on the breakdown of the family, is already
being reflected in officially sanctioned and distributed documents on parenting.
As Karen noted,

There's all this stuff around at the moment from the government
about parenting and 'good' parenting. There's obviously a sort of push
on that. (*Karen*)

And the message that is being conveyed is of parental responsibility for ensuring that children do as they are told, which reflects the change in emphasis in
schooling. The intention is, of course, that this will feed through into ideologies
of parenting. Such attempts at social engineering are, perhaps, inevitably
doomed to failure because they depend upon, at least, a degree of consensus and
a shared world-view. This is a state of affairs which, it is now widely recognized,
can no longer be realistically expected. As Ken Plummer notes, 'the call to
return to "traditional values" or "family values" or to get "back to basics", is a
call that has no grasp of modernity'.[14] Nevertheless, hegemonies can exert an
influence even if only insofar as they provide a standard against which large
numbers of people can be seen to fail.

Any changes that do result will take time to filter through, although the
demand that teachers teach the National Curriculum has led to some differences in practice, if not in attitudes. I was trained, however, both as a teacher
and as a mother, according to the child-centred models and so, to a greater or

lesser extent, were all the primary-school teachers I interviewed. Some were acutely conscious of the extent to which they had been influenced:

> I was very influenced by Plowden. I was brought up on Plowden, that was my bible at the time. And it sticks. I suppose if I had to go back into schools it still would be. And it's about the whole child, as you know, and it's about not missing any opportunity to give them learning experiences. So you'd tend not just to walk them to the baths for their swimming lesson, you'd tend to say, 'Now, let's have a look at this shop here. Now what does it sell? What's the proper name for this? It's not a cake shop. What's the proper word? Is it confectioners? Bakers?' Extending their vocabulary, counting things. It's exhausting. (*Lesley*)

> I was trained according to the Plowden philosophy. It was very much about developing the children as individuals, starting from where they were, using their interests, so it was the child-centred sort of thing. . . . I saw my job as being about building a relationship with the children and obviously there was the reading and writing, the basic skills, but also sort of developing them as people, for them to look at how they related to people. . . . Which I still feel, that's still my philosophy . . . but on a sort of broader perspective. (*Karen*)

Some people were acutely conscious of what alternative approaches to those suggested by Plowden might involve. Abida, for example, had experience of an extremely didactic approach to early years education, while others were suspicious of the implications that the National Curriculum had for their preferred pedagogical style:

> When I came to put my son into nursery I wasn't very impressed or happy with what I saw. So, I read quite a lot of books from the British Council which all talked of Plowden type, child-centred approaches and I decided that I'd like to open a nursery school for very young children, as their first experience where they would be happy because all the schools I'd checked out, they weren't happy and the whole environment was like a grown-up school. Just chairs put out straight and very little equipment and books and pencils and writing just so . . . in fact I stopped my son from getting promoted to the next school. She said, 'Help him at home with his alphabet', I said, 'Look, just leave him alone. Just let him play around. I'm quite happy with that. I don't want to push him into reading and writing. He'll be OK. He'll catch up. Don't worry. You don't worry. I'm not.' So I built a nursery for twenty-five kids in my backyard with windows at the right height and loads of toys. . . . I bought loads of stuff in England and people came and they liked it because they'd never seen anything like it before. . . .

My style was very different. But we still had to train them to get into school. We had to prepare them for the tests that schools gave out at 5-plus, which was that they had to know their English alphabet, capital and small letters. That they had to write three-letter words and be given dictation on them . . . they must know plus and minus sums up to ten. They must know their numbers from one to 100 and they must know their Urdu. Again, they must be able to write their alphabet and write small letters and be given dictation. So, despite the fact that I disagreed with having to teach children so much formal work when they're not really ready, when they're a little older they do the same work within a week or two weeks, so I tried to take as much pressure off the children as possible, tried to slow it down but still, nevertheless, still have to prepare them for their schools. (*Abida*)

I worry about children now, with the National Curriculum, and especially with the SATS. I know that we try to make it as natural as possible but there are those who get upset. I'm just glad that my children missed it. I actually think I'd be inclined to take them out when they were doing the tests, I don't think they have a place in primary education. . . . When they first bought it [National Curriculum] in I was concerned that we'd lose those spontaneous chances that you get, a kid brings something in and you go off on a whole project about it because it's interesting and you can see all these learning opportunities with it. Well I think we did a bit but Dearing will help, I think we convinced them we were right with that one, and anyway we managed to work it out. But if you're not careful, too much what I call formal work can intrude on your relationships. (*Sylvia*)

Plowden was concerned with the primary years and so far I have only quoted the views of primary teachers but even those who opted for secondary courses were aware of what Hilary Burgess and Bob Carter[15] have called the 'Mumsy' ideology of primary teaching. In fact it was her knowledge of how she would be expected to espouse this as a primary teacher which put Gillian off becoming one:

Before you start your PGCE you have to spend two weeks in a primary school and the head there actually said I ought to have done primary, but how you can tell after two weeks there, I don't know. But I'm glad I didn't now. I don't think I could stand to be in a classroom with all these little children . . . and all this making things. I don't mind making things with Robert but no, I couldn't see myself as a sort of story-time person, 'Let's all gather round and Mummy teacher here will read you a story.' I'm not really that sort. (*Gillian*)

A TWO-WAY EXCHANGE: PARENT–TEACHER, TEACHER–PARENT

So, how did other teachers perceive and experience this ideology of teacher as mother? What did it mean for them at school with their pupils and at home with their own children? And how did the fact that they were themselves 'real' mothers fit in?

In official documents dealing with the selection of candidates for teacher training considerable emphasis is placed on personal characteristics. Teresa was in agreement with this thinking.

> I knew that I couldn't work with reception age children. I think you need special qualities for that and I don't think I've got them. I'm certainly not patient enough, though I'm better than I was before I had Christopher. I would have liked to have done secondary but I wasn't sure that I had the sort of emotional strength that you need for that. I remember what I was like in secondary school, I'm not sure I could have coped with that. And the sort of schools I wanted to work in, I wasn't sure that I would be capable of putting up with the sort of treatment you're likely to get. So, that left me with junior. . . . I was watching Christopher's teacher really closely because I thought, what's she going to be like? Is he going to be happy there? And she's actually brilliant because she's so laid back that she lets it all wash over her and she's still a good teacher. He's learning such a lot and he's only been there five or six weeks and he's coming on really well. So I think you need a certain attitude but it's got to be inherent. You can't learn it. It's got to be something that's there already, and she's got it, but a lot of people haven't. (*Teresa*)

Patience was almost inevitably cited as an essential characteristic. The saying that 'Patience is a virtue' perhaps gives some indication of how it doesn't often come naturally to people. All the mother teachers I spoke with told me that they had had to develop their capacity to be patient and tolerant in order to cope with life with their own children:

> I'm more patient – the kids would howl with laughter if they heard this – I'm more patient. I'm more realistic in my expectations of what children can do and what you can ask them to do that they don't think they can do. . . . I suppose it's realism sets in, that there are some things that are just unattainable but you can still ask them to have a crack at it as long as you promote it properly. . . . I certainly think I'm better at knowing how to see that it isn't like a brick wall in front of them . . . because I've had enormous trouble with my son and his confidence since his best friend died. (*Doreen*)

I think it's made me a lot more tolerant of children and where they're at and how they feel, even though my two have been extremely bright . . . and been able to have lots of opportunities to join in lots of things . . . but it still makes me understand what it's like when something goes wrong. (*Sylvia*)

I've realized that they need more time just for growing up, I think. I used to think that they were more adult than they were and having children you realize that they are not these adults, that they are still children. (*Gillian*)

Father teachers also talked about how they had become more tolerant as a result of their experiences with their own children:

I guess that somewhere along the line it's made me much more tolerant towards individuals because you become more aware of individual circumstances. I'm much more patient, much more tolerant. Whether you would develop anyway with just more experience, more dealings with kids, and as you teach more there's less confrontation, more chance for it, I don't know, but I do think that it's having Sean and Ruby and having to learn to adjust to their pace, in everything, that's just brought it home to me. (*James*)

I've been able to talk to them and not feel as if I was teaching them a lot more. I've seen them as human and not thinking, well, this lesson I've got to teach this, this and this, and get that across and if they open their mouths to talk about anything else you shut them up quickly. Just at the start of the day, when the kids come in, before you actually teach them, I used to begrudge that a bit but I've been quite glad of it [lately] because they come in, they've talked, not about their lessons, they just talk about themselves. And you find out a surprising lot; you know, a lad says his father's moved out and his mother's had to look after them and all this business. And you can be very sympathetic to what they do in the rest of the day then. (*Chris*)

I'm not a very patient person at all but I think I'm a bit more so since I had the kids. Yes, definitely. Because you have to be. It's no use getting yourself worked up and in a state, perhaps you learn to be more patient as a sort of survival strategy. I do still get impatient but I think I'm not quite so bad and other people tell me I'm not. (*Stuart*)

Associated with patience is understanding. Gillian and Karen both felt that they had become much more 'mellow' and relaxed, and, perhaps, less idealistic than their child-free colleagues:

When I was still at school I went into an infant class once a week to help out and that was it. I knew that that was exactly what I wanted to do . . . infants are just full of wonder, like doing nice things, talk to you, you can talk to them and I thought, I want to spend my time with these little people . . . just step in and have fun. . . . When I started teaching I loved my class. They were like friends. But of course, I was always one step away, I was in charge. Yes, I enjoyed their company intensely. In fact I much preferred to sit at their table with them at lunch than with the other bitter and fed-up teachers. (*Helen*)

Karen had a similar view:

What I really enjoyed, and this I think is why I never went into secondary teaching, because what I really enjoyed was having a class that you formed relationships with and you were with those children, good and bad, but yeah, I enjoyed being with them and I enjoyed their spontaneity . . . someone brought something in and you'd suddenly do a whole topic on it or something. (*Karen*)

It is obviously not necessary to be a parent to love and care for children but what was interesting was the frequency with which parent teachers said that their loving and caring became more intense when they had their own, because they saw them reflected in their pupils. My feelings, which led to me doing this research were not, therefore, unusual:

I used to like being with children but it was never something I wanted to do permanently until I had my own children. . . . You can't help but put your own kids in. I put Nicola in every time when there's a lack of confidence because no way will I ever allow a quiet child to be overlooked because I know what my own daughter's gone through. So you can see that some of the theory does tie in and you can latch on to it because you've experienced it and you don't want that to happen to anyone else's because you know what it's been like for your own child. You know how they come home and how upset they can be. . . . One day I was talking to a boy about his work and he just stood there, the same way as [my son] does and I knew that this little boy was frightened and I just said to him, 'Look, I'm not going to shout at you. I just want to talk about it. Let's see what we can do', and he just cried. And I thought, you should divorce yourself away from it. But you think, God, that's my child that's happening to, so, you can't help it . . . my heart just went out to him so I picked him up and gave him a cuddle. (*Katie*)

Since we had our daughter I can't help getting upset about children being upset. My husband can't even watch anything on the television about cruelty to children. It's too easy to identify it with your own child or perhaps it's not that, perhaps knowledge of your own child widens your feelings towards other children. It's hard to identify. (*Nicola*)

In certain ways . . . I've made closer bonds and had a better relationship with, maybe 5-year-olds, 6-year-olds, than I would have done or would ever have made the effort to do before. I'm prepared to see them much more as interesting little individuals whereas I'm sure that, at one time, when I was 22 maybe, if they didn't read the *Guardian* they were a waste of time. They've got very interesting little personalities, even by the time they're 5 or 6, and they're all different. (*James*)

I think I like children more than I did. I think I was more likely to objectify them and think they were just little objects that could be moulded into what I wanted them to be. I think I probably get on with them better. . . . I definitely feel more protective towards them, you can't help it and it can be quite obstructive because there are times, especially on TP, when some of the kids have personal problems at home. One little boy's mother had run off with a neighbour and he was such a lovely boy but he didn't do any work and I should have been stricter with him than I was, but I was only there for five weeks though, so it wasn't really my place to try and enforce some discipline. . . . He didn't do any work, he didn't try and stop anyone else from working. And I just wanted to take him home, he was so nice. . . . You just can't help feeling sorry for them, even though you try to be professional. (*Teresa*)

I was always particularly conscious of children's safety after I'd had my own children because I could always think, if this is L or S, especially if the child physically resembled my child, which some of them did. So, in the early days, for example, if I was on playground duty and a child came and complained, 'He's hitting me, he's thumping me, he's calling me names', and all that . . . I'd say, 'Oh, go away. For goodness' sake don't. Stop this. I don't want to know.' After I'd had children of my own I could empathize with them and I did think, yes, this poor child. If this were my child I would want someone to take notice of it. And that's the difference in that I was able to think that much more vicariously, and consider that these are human beings, they've got feelings and you've got to be really, really careful, overcautious, more cautious with other people's children than you are with your own. I was just as strict but I was a lot more careful. (*Lesley*)

Having your own children must change the way you see children. . . .
You get an understanding of children but you don't really know where
you get it from or how you get it. . . . I think having a child of my own
helped. And I'm sure I must be more understanding than when I first
started to teach. (*Ann*)

Since I've had Richard I feel more demonstrative than I did. Like you
can get hold of one and give them a hug which perhaps you can't
before you've had your own. Perhaps some people can but I was an
only one. Perhaps if you're from a different sort of family. (*Jane*)

Yes, I do like children more now. Well, I think it's almost inevitable
really. I can't say that I find other people's children easy to talk with
but now, if someone brings a baby into school I do like to hold them
and have a cuddle and I would never ever have done that before.
(*Stuart*)

I think I have gradually come to see pupils differently . . . at the
beginning really there's a tendency to assert some superiority over
them, when you first start teaching, when you're young, I suppose,
but I tend to feel rather sorry for them now. . . . I suppose inevitably,
whether I do it consciously or not, I see my own children in them
really. (*Margery*)

One way of interpreting what these teachers are saying is that once they
had their own children their professional knowledge, consciousness and practice was, to some extent, altered. It was no longer possible for them to 'other' or,
as Teresa put it, to 'objectify' their pupils. That is, they could not see them as
separate, distinct and different beings. Their theoretical understanding was
humanized by their practical and immediate knowledge of their own children at
home. Emotion had intruded on the professional picture.

Of course, everyone's theoretical knowledge is rudely challenged the first
time they set foot in a classroom regardless of whether or not they have their
own children. Most people have to make adjustments in the light of experience
because theory is, by definition, abstract and general and is premised on ideal
cases. However, the parent teachers felt that many of their adjustments were of
a different order to those which resulted from what might be characterized as
professional first encounters or 'critical incidents'.[18] This is because they arose
from a personal and emotional feeling, some called it a gut feeling, of identification of their pupils with their own children. Grumet puts it in the following
words: 'Our relations to other people's children are inextricably linked to our
relation to our own progeny, actual and possible, and to the attribution of rights
and influences that we attribute to that affiliation'.[19] Thus it was not just a
straightforward matter of becoming more familiar with and fond of kids since,

for anyone, getting to know children as their teacher means getting to know them as people and may even mean coming to love them. Strong emotional ties are often involved[20] and, as Steedman notes,[21] plenty of (women) teachers are 'seduced by the pressure of little fingers' and, like Steedman herself, have made a conscious decision not to be mothers themselves. I have known teachers who have chosen to dedicate themselves to their pupils because, for various reasons, they preferred having the care of and opportunity to love many children to having their own, personal family. Initially this was Helen's thinking:

> I wouldn't say it was a substitute but I felt that if you had a job where you were working with children well, that would be enough. And it was at first. . . . I had no thoughts about having children at all. (*Helen*)

Indeed, until the marriage bars which prohibited married women being employed as teachers were repealed in 1944, women often did have to choose between their own and other people's children. No such demands were made on men because their marital and parental role was not conceived of as being so home based or as immediate to the welfare and nurturance of their children. 'Proper' husbands and fathers went out to work and left the bulk of the housework and child care to their wives. They would have been seen as failing in their task if they had done otherwise. These notions of 'correctness' and propriety regarding the role, contribution and attitude of effective parents and teachers are central to the respective dominant ideologies of teaching and parenting and do, therefore, need to be considered critically. It is especially important to do this because, in a number of respects, they bear little resemblance to the lived experience of many people.

THE VALUE ACCORDED TO PARENTAL EXPERIENCE

For a start, ironically, neither experientially based understanding nor the significance of personally felt emotion has traditionally been given much status or currency within the formal and official accounts of what mothers and teachers are supposed to do and feel. Indeed, the workings of a politics of emotions means that teachers who wish to be seen as 'professionals', even professionals according to the mother-made-conscious model, may be reluctant to admit to feelings which have maternal associations. This leads to further devaluation for, as Grumet writes,

> by withholding information about that relation [between mother and child] from the public discourse of educational theory we deny our own experience and our own knowledge. Our silence certifies the system and we become complicit with theorists and teachers who repudiate the intimacy of nurture in their own histories and their work in education.[22]

I say this is ironic because since the 1960s, and especially following Plowden, considerable emphasis has been placed on the importance, for educational success, of the role of the mother, of home–school links and of partnership with parents. Given this, one could be excused for thinking that parental knowledge would be valued. But this has not been the case because, as Cortazzi[23] demonstrates, teachers have been encouraged to think in terms of 'teacher' and 'parent' as polarized binary oppositions. On this view teachers are the 'experts' who, possessing professional knowledge, know more about children, and by implication, individual children, than parents do. Teachers are exhorted to find out as much as they can about a child's home background in order to gain a better understanding of what will expedite that child's learning. Plowden was quite explicit about what might have to be done as a result of such knowledge: 'When children are materially, intellectually or emotionally deprived, teachers must strive to serve as substitutes for parents'.[24] This was by no means a new view, nor was it always confined to children who might be considered to be socially deprived. As Tyler[25] shows, a social pathology perspective in which mothers (but rarely fathers) are seen as deficient and actually responsible for damaging perfect children has a long and a continuing history. Indeed a deficit view of women and mothers can be shown to have influenced the curriculum for girls in general and working-class girls in particular throughout the existence of state-funded education.[26]

PARENT TEACHERS' PERCEPTIONS OF PARENTS

So, while primary teachers are required to adopt a particular type of 'motherly' approach they are also encouraged to see themselves as professionals with expert knowledge *vis à vis* their pupils' parents. When the teachers are themselves parents this can lead to some critical questioning of the dominant ideologies in which they have been trained as teachers and as mothers. Once again, what happens is that the messiness of experience and reality comes up against the neatness and clarity of rhetoric. It is also the case that acceptance of the dominant views places mother teachers in an extremely difficult position. This is because their professional training has taught them that, as mothers, they are liable to damage their own children: yet, at the same time, as teachers they are reckoned to have total responsibility as substitute mothers for a whole class of children. Seen like this it is almost impossible for them to succeed. As Walkerdine and Lucey note, the likely outcome is that,

> women teachers are burdened with guilt. They simultaneously blame parents for children's failure and blame themselves, since the other fiction is that 'correct development' should be ensured through adequate knowledge and monitoring of each child.[27]

Nicola, Sylvia and Karen dealt with this by becoming less willing to be censorious and to adopt a pathological perspective on parents:

Before you're a mother you say, 'Oh! I'd never let my child do that!', and when you are a mother you realize that, oh yes you probably would because there are worse things that they could do. (*Nicola*)

I'm not as judgemental I think, because I can now see reasons why people don't do things 'properly'. (*Sylvia*)

One thing I've noticed over the years, people who aren't parents will say things like, 'Well, why aren't the parents doing this?', you know, 'Why is . . . ?' And those teachers who are parents can actually see that perhaps there are other things, the complexities of the family and home life. That life isn't black and white really, but that all sorts of things go on within the family. (*Karen*)

Jane, who had been a single parent in difficult circumstances, found herself being much more sympathetic:

It meant that you appreciated the mother's role more whereas I think, when you're a young teacher you don't appreciate that because you've not been in that position yourself . . . but you appreciate mum's role and mum's relationship and sometimes the fact that she feels fed up and that sort of thing and sometimes there's problems at home and sometimes she doesn't like that child for some reason . . . because I don't think that enters your head really, when you're young, or when you're not a mum yourself rather. (*Jane*)

Being a parent also makes teachers more aware of the sorts of concerns people have when they hand their children over to the care of the school. Cortazzi suggests that teachers perceive a significant minority of parents as being 'awkward' and that this minority may affect their perceptions and experiences of the majority.[28] Parent teachers, however, seemed to be less likely to perceive other parents as awkward, difficult and obstructive when they questioned procedures and practices. They were more able to see their point of view, especially, perhaps, if the root of the difficulty was perceived as being a teacher who was childless:

If there are children with problems in school, the teachers that haven't got children say, 'Parents! Ruddy parents! They ought to make sure blah, blah, blah.' But those of us who have say, 'But it's not like that.' So it's good to have people on the staff to counter that thinking about 'proper parenting', that people who aren't parents see parenting as a very sort of simple thing, whereas if you do this, this and this your child will be all right. Which is also a pressure on parents who are teachers when their own children are in trouble because you feel, 'Oh God! I ought to be a good parent, I ought to be even better.' (*Karen*)

Mrs — [head teacher at my first school] was very cagey about parents in schools. She said that it was an open school and it was in the brochure that parents were always welcome but that wasn't really the case. I just don't think that she wanted them to see what we were doing. And we didn't send much work home either. I was told not to do it. Parents could come in but it had to be very formal, at the same time every week and for the whole year. I didn't realize at the time how difficult it is to make a commitment like that. Anyway I was told that parents could organize the book corner and wash paint brushes, do baking and that sort of thing but we weren't to use them to listen to reading. I was a bit surprised about that because it would have been helpful to say the least. The reason was that they wouldn't do it properly, they'd make wrong prompts and things like that. I know that's rubbish because you can tell parents what you want them to do, some schools do training sessions. And anyway this school is in the most middle-class area in —. I knew people in other schools who used to say it must be like working in a private school at —. And I think this was at the root of it. She thought these parents were difficult middle-class parents who were likely to be critical. She hasn't got any children, through her own choice, and you can tell. Everyone who's got kids says the same, you can tell. I think that now. I'm appalled at how I was but I accepted it. Thinking back I remember mutterings from the teachers who had got their own kids but they kept it quiet, they had to do what she said and she kept a very close watch. Perhaps they did things differently in the classroom with the parents when they were in, I don't know because they'd have to keep it very quiet. If that was Andrew's school I'd be seriously thinking about withdrawing him and I'm sure she wouldn't be like that if she had her own. She's only concerned with her career and I think she will do very well, but she doesn't have the personal experience of children and of being a parent that I think is essential now that I've got my own. (*Janice*)

I remember, before I had children, a good friend of mine talking about her little boy who'd just started school, in reception. And she had dreadful trouble and she kept going up to the school to complain. She's a teacher as well. He didn't want to go to school and all this, that and the other. And the upshot of it was that she felt that the reception teacher (and she's a reception teacher herself), was too strict with them. She said, 'She's too strict for reception.' And, at the time I'd got no children, and I thought, oh, I don't see as that's the case. You've got to be strict with children sometimes. Especially knowing her child, Nigel's a little bugger you know, so I thought well, I'd be strict with him. I didn't say anything but I thought, he deserves it. So, had I been teaching reception I could well have been that teacher about who she complained, until I had my own. And then, after I'd had my own I actually was in the position, several times, of teaching reception as a support teacher, but I still had a lot of responsibility. And her words came back to me and I thought well, damn it all, that was important. I could really see them, this is their first day at school. Well? Whereas normally, before I had children I'd have probably said, 'Goodness me child! Sit down', you know, this sort of thing, 'What do you think you're doing walking about? You don't walk about in school.' And then of course it's obvious, when you've had children of your own, it's a big trauma for these poor things. I mean you've got to really bed them in gently. So certainly, in that respect, it made me a lot more aware and I was a lot more considerate of how parents felt about things and less ready to brush them off as awkward parents. (*Lesley*)

But it is not just teachers who negatively see parents as their opposites: it works both ways. Being aware of this, some teachers used their status as parents to establish a point of contact and to forge what they saw as more real and realistic links. This tactic seemed to be of especial importance to those in working-class areas where parents are often not comfortable in schools or with teachers:

It's helped me a great deal in conversation with them, like if they come with a problem and I can say, 'Oh, when Catherine was little.' That really does help because they then see that you've gone through all that. And if you can say, 'Oh well, wait till they're a teenager, I've got some right problems at the moment', that gives them a bit more confidence really, to tackle things. (*Sylvia*)

I have found that, being a head, parents will come to talk to me about things because they know I'm a parent and if we are talking I'll say, 'Well, my child, when my child was', and immediately they're thinking, 'Well, you know', and so I think it gives you some credibility with the parents and especially if I can say, 'Well, my son was in trouble and I had to go up to the school', or something, and they're thinking, 'Oh, it happens to you as well.' So I find it a great help. (*Karen*)

I do think that having had a daughter has made a tremendous difference to my work with parents because, in the FE tradition one doesn't
have a lot of contact with parents but I do, for half my timetable is
with youngsters with learning difficulties and I'm a tutor for the
course for students with learning difficulties so one's relating to parents far more closely than one is in the traditional FE setting. So that
helps tremendously. I would have little credibility with them if I
wasn't a parent myself. . . . I think it does help. It gives me credibility
as a human being. (*Rebecca*)

On one level, by establishing common ground these teachers can be seen as
rejecting both the orthodoxy and their status as 'experts'. Rebecca, for instance,
who taught in a college of further education, did this explicitly by using her position as a mother to gain credibility with some of her students:

I was teaching other mothers, so there was a common bond with
teaching other women, many of whom were returning to learning,
their families having grown up. The fact that I could speak as one who
had been at home and was now going back to work myself, I found
incredibly useful. It did give us a common language. . . . I used to
make a point of mentioning that I had a young daughter and a husband and a home to keep as well because it gave credibility and status
to their own position as housewives, that this wasn't something that I
neglected or hadn't chosen, or considered unimportant: that it was an
important part of my life. (*Rebecca*)

PARENT TEACHERS IN MANAGEMENT

Karen and Sylvia were both head teachers and so were in a position to take
things even further and to make organizational and structural arrangements
which accommodated their views on motherhood. For example, on the basis of
their own experience they always took account of some of the practical difficulties mothers and fathers face in coming to school and being seen to be supportive of their children. They knew that not being able to come to morning
assemblies or to attend workshops did not necessarily mean that parents did
not care:

You immediately think about your own circumstances; and the particular thing that's happened here that's been influenced by my own
circumstances was we kept trying to get parents in, or particular
mothers in, during the day and I remembered the pressure that I
think my own children felt at school when they'd come home and say,
'Everybody's mummy was in, except you', and I thought that was an
awful pressure to be putting on the children when there were so many

parents who just cannot do that during the day. So we eased right off that and I looked at other ways that would fit in with people's working and family lives. (*Karen*)

It's taught me a lot about things like workshops, because you can't assume that parents are there for workshops. . . . I always think of my own position and I wasn't able, as a working mum, to do that; I think it's made me more understanding of a mum's point of view, or a parent's point of view. (*Sylvia*)

They also appreciated the difficulties the mother teachers on their staff sometimes faced when their own children needed them. As Rebecca said,

I like working with other married women and other mothers, especially when they are the ones in charge because, working as I've done all the time while my daughter was at school, if I phoned in and said, 'My daughter's got measles' then fine. There's never been any 'Oh well, you'll need to find someone to look after her while you come in.' There's been an automatic acceptance that she came first. (*Rebecca*)

This sort of response is so very different from that experienced by Gillian when her male head teacher docked her pay while her son was in hospital. Mother heads recognize the way in which, out of necessity, many women develop the ability to juggle their lives:

The women I work with seem to interweave all the threads of their lives so that they can go from teaching, say Elizabethan history, fly down to the shop and get the bread for tea tonight, come back, mark essays; whereas a man has to do the teaching, do the marking, and perhaps get the bread on the way home. I can stir the stew and plan tomorrow's lesson at the same time. . . . It may be a skill that women develop through expectations on us. (*Rebecca*)

Women can do more things at once. They have to. Women don't usually have the luxury of being able to focus on just one thing, and it's not just working women who have to do it. If you're looking after children and running a home then, unless you're very strict, and I don't think you can be, you'll be doing something, the kids come in, they demand attention, you have to deal with it then get on with what you're doing in the first place. Men, or at least the ones I know, don't do that. They say, 'Go away, I'm busy, I can't concentrate.' You can try saying that as a mum but it won't work. (*Ann*)

As head teachers, Karen and Sylvia clearly valued the knowledge and experience that parent teachers brought to their work:

> When I first came here most of the staff were married but didn't have children and I thought that was absolutely obvious – the way that they treated children, the way they would give them a good ten-minute dressing down on something that was so minimal, that you'd have said, 'Now, you stop that', and go on to your next thing. But as time's gone on most have retired and it's changed and I've added my ethos to things. . . . We've only got one married member who's not got children and I think over the years her attitude has gradually changed. She referred to it as a culture shock, coming here and meeting these parents and I know what she meant in one way; but when you've had your own children something prepares you for the fact that it won't all be like the adverts on the TV about this happy little family eating round the table, and I can see how she's developed but she's still very cold with children. (*Sylvia*)

By her 'own ethos' Sylvia was also alluding to the way in which, when interviewing prospective staff, she did take into account how they behaved with children, and their empathy with and understanding of the difficulties experienced by parents living in the economically depressed, one-time mining village. To her mind, teachers who were themselves parents tended to be the ones she wanted for her school because they were the people with the 'right' characteristics and attitudes. Ian, another head teacher, said much the same thing:

> Mrs S is a good teacher but she'll be even better when she's had a child of her own. At the moment she is a bit cold and distant with the children. I've seen lots of people who were like that change as soon as they had a baby. I don't suppose I should be saying this because you'll have me down as sexist but I think it's true. It's true of men too, but not in quite the same way because they have a different sort of relationship with kids anyway. I can't quite put my finger on it, but if you talk to most heads they'll tell you the same, I'm sure. (*Ian*)

While it is heartening to know that not all head teachers are prejudiced against mothers, Ian is right in implying that he is getting onto dangerous ground by suggesting that, as primary teachers, they are in some way superior to child-free women. For a start, he is making rather a sweeping generalization which condemns people who are involuntarily childless. Nevertheless having children does, inevitably, change people and changes the sort of teacher they are. James was quite surprised at the extent to which one of the deputy heads at his school had changed once he became a father relatively late in life:

There's one person in whom I've seen a great change since he had children. His attitude towards teachers and work and teachers who were parents and work outside school time has changed beyond recognition, along with his expectations of teachers that were parents who've got a different set of imperatives: he's changed totally. It's more marked than in anyone I've ever seen. He's been more sympathetic in a lot of situations in different ways. (*James*)

Thinking back, Lesley found that her 'models' had been mother teachers:

At my first school, hardly any of them had children, the school where they were really bad with the children, and the two staff, they were older ladies, who were most considerate and kind to the children, they were the ones who had grown-up children of their own. . . . I think it's probably fair to say that I've developed a lot of professionality . . . in terms of teacher craft knowledge and professional skills. That's been mainly through example, through watching experienced, what I thought were competent colleagues. And all the ones whom I've wanted to emulate have been mothers and the ones who I wouldn't have wanted to, haven't had children. (*Lesley*)

PARENT TEACHERS AND 'CULTURAL REPRODUCTION'

But it is not just with regard to the way in which parents *per se* are characterized within the Plowdenesque, child-centred ideology that some teachers began to question what they had been encouraged to take for granted. Numerous critics and commentators have demonstrated and discussed the extent to which the ideology reflects specific historical, social and cultural values. Essentially these values are 'middle-class', male and eurocentric, and these are the values that teachers are expected to pass on and reproduce. If they are to stand in as parents then they are to be middle-class ones. Being concerned with the early socialization at least as much as the academic learning of their pupils, primary-school teachers have frequently been described as being heavily implicated in this process of cultural reproduction.[29] Working in a school which served a predominantly Asian population, Karen was acutely aware of the dilemmas and possibilities:

We actually did a lot of work last year. We were working with the Community Education Development Centre looking at parenting, so we were doing work with the children and also work with their parents as well, and that was very interesting because we were talking about what we did in school; but they started talking about their own childhood and what their perceptions of what a teacher and a school is and, you know, it's very different. Very different. Particularly for those who grew up in India or Pakistan, it's very much 'Get in there, the teacher teaches, the children do it.' Very much a more masculine type of a model. So that was very interesting for us, but also for them, for us to talk about how we approach it. But it's a very Anglo Saxon, white sort of thing and I think that puts a lot of pressure on parents. We were very careful when we were doing this work with the parents not to say, 'This is right. This is how it should be.' We actually let them talk about issues they've got with being a parent and not denigrating, but saying, 'There are different sorts of family. Every family's valid.' But I think it is hard because it's not only from schools, it's the media and everything. They're bombarded by these images of the perfect family. (*Karen*)

A key feature of the dominant perspective is the separation of what have been characterized as the personal and professional or the public and private aspects of life. Some feminists have argued that such a separation is antithetical to women's lived experience and to the way in which women make sense of and conceptualize the world. In my view it is essentially the same for men and becoming a father may serve as a catalyst for the realization that this is indeed the case. It certainly seems that, once they become parents, it is not as easy for teachers to make any such artificial separation because they deal with and have knowledge of children in both spheres, at home and at work. At least this was the case for those with whom I talked. One consequence of this seems to be that, although in some respects the outcome of their work may be seen as cultural reproduction, they have thought critically and deliberately about what they do and why they do it. At the root of their deliberations is their tendency to constantly reflect their own children back onto their pupils. Thus, the question that is always in their minds is, Would I want this for my child? They are, therefore, casting themselves in a parental role *vis à vis* their pupils. I found no evidence of the sort of thinking leading to the approach that Steedman describes in terms of,

> the mild and genteel methods by which working-class children are led to see – out of what kind and painful necessity it is done! – that, really, they aren't very clever, really, can never be like their teacher's own child at home . . . the main perpetrators are mainly women.[30]

This is not to say that such teachers are not about. It may be that, in England and Wales, teacher thinking has, over the last twenty-five to thirty years been influenced by the notion of equality of opportunity and by a predominantly comprehensive education system to the extent that teachers are as likely to attribute educational success to opportunity and access as they are to 'cleverness'. Of course, the fact that I didn't come across this view may equally be to do with the composition of my 'sample', or with their desire to give 'socially acceptable' accounts. Inevitably, comparisons were made between the teachers' own children and their pupils but in these 'luck' was seen as the major factor:

> I think that you realize that [pupils] have these home lives and some-
> times just coming to school is a big thing for some of these children if
> their home lives are really desperate. And I don't think I took that into
> account before I had my two. I really think these two are lucky. They've
> got all the things they could possibly want. They've got two parents that
> love them and that love each other. I think some children go to school
> and they must feel, well, I don't know how they must feel. (*Gillian*)

Taking this view a number of teachers said that their main aim was to help children to 'beat the system' and to do better than might stereotypically be expected
for someone of their social class, gender or ethnicity. There is, perhaps
inevitably, an element of 'colonialism' here insofar as the notion of 'doing better'
implies a value judgement. However, to say that this equals cultural reproduction, and that this is a 'bad thing' is too simplistic an interpretation. Most parents want their children to have every opportunity and to do better than they
themselves did and, in becoming a parent teacher the people I talked with also
felt this keenly for their pupils. This led to some of them rejecting the dominant
ideologies (of mothering and primary teaching) as being likely to result in reproduction, despite the rhetoric that they will lead to the optimum development of
each child's potential.

Helen, for instance, was concerned about the issue of discipline:

> I found the very child-centred, very non-directive philosophy that I
> was trained in very unhelpful when it came to discipline because it
> seemed there [at the second school I worked in] that it was contrary.
> You had to be very open in what you were teaching and how you were
> organizing it, and yet you had to be very firm and directive when it
> came to discipline if they were actually to learn anything. It's very dif-
> ficult to do both because when you're actually teaching, when it's your
> class, you're doing both all the time, you're switching in and out of
> those. (*Helen*)

Helen had worked in schools in both comfortable, middle-class areas and in a
very deprived working-class estate. In the former the children knew how the
school expected them to behave and they were able to get on with learning in an
environment that was not dissimilar to that at home. For the other children,
however, school was, in many respects, very different to home and this could
make things difficult for them and for their teachers. In these circumstances
Helen and others have found that a more didactic and openly teacher-directed
approach works better because it is not based on the mistaken assumption that
children will respond in a particular, 'natural' manner.

Learning is about changing and adapting as a result of experience. Helen, I and all other parent teachers have the advantage of first-hand experience with their own children which gives us an additional perspective that can, if we let it, add a certain depth and a roundness to our work. I can see, and to some extent agree with the point that Gitlin and Myers are making when they write, that

> there is a fundamental connection between educating and rearing children: however it is a denied and devalued connection because it is gender-related. When we are educating, we are rearing, but women are expected to educate in ways that contradict our ways of rearing and what we know about living and being with children. The rearing of children involves intimacy and nurturance . . . school, on the other hand, is a place of control and compliance. . . . Rather than fostering intimacy and nurturance, relationships in schools centre around theories of expertise and authority leading to a sense of detachment and isolation.[31]

However, whilst acknowledging the structural constraints that militate against intimacy and nurturance, the parent teachers I spoke with all felt that, in their own dealings with pupils, they were able to develop and foster these characteristics. They were able to bring what they had personally learnt as mothers to bear upon their practice. Gillian sums up what this means for her:

> I think being a good teacher is similar to being a good mother. You've got to have time for them and if they want to talk to you then you've got to let them talk to you. They've got all this baggage that comes with them and you've got to get over that before you can actually start to teach them. I think you've got to discipline them. I think it's probably exactly the same role really. You're disciplining them, you're giving them the boundaries. I'm probably quite free in the classroom but they know what they can't do and what they can do. I call my sixth form my babies, even to their face. 'And how are my babies today?' And I suppose you do nurture them, especially as you teach them through school and you've had them from third year (Year 9) perhaps . . . and you watch them grow, watch them develop and watch them change. You get quite proud of them really. They're doing their A-levels this year and it was me that was taking them through.
> I really regretted [leaving them for maternity leave]. I know that I really wanted Sarah, but I really regretted not being there. I felt so guilty about not being there and I've given them my phone number so that they can phone me up or whatever. I know I shouldn't. I've told them not to tell anybody. But yes, I suppose they are. It's exactly the same role I would say. (*Gillian*)

Grumet suggests that

> reproducing ourselves also brings a critical dimension to biological and ideological reproduction by suggesting the reflexive capacity of parents to reconceive our own childhoods and education as well as our own situation as adults and to choose another way for ourselves expressed in the nurture of our progeny. . . . Curriculum becomes our way of contradicting biology and ideology.[32]

For teachers in the United Kingdom and in much of the world, prescribed curricula, pedagogy and organizational structures together with internalized values and beliefs do limit, but not prohibit, the individual's ability to mount a challenge. However, the evidence does suggest that the emotional contribution that parenthood in general and motherhood in particular makes to teachers' sense of themselves does influence their practice and that this influence is not necessarily of quite the same order as that expected by the official ideology of 'teacher as parent'. The difference may only be slight but to the teachers themselves it lies, significantly, in the difference between theory and practice.

NOTES

1   Clarke, K., 'Public and Private Children: Infant Education in the 1820s and 1830s', in Steedman, C. Urwin, C. and Walkerdine, V. (eds), *Language, Gender and Childhood,* London, Routledge & Kegan Paul, 1985.
2   Casey, K., *I Answer With My Life: Life Histories of Women Teachers Working For Social Change,* New York, Routledge, 1993, pp. 84f.
3   See Connell, R., *Teachers' Work,* Sydney, Allen & Unwin, 1985; Huberman, M., *The Lives of Teachers* (trans. J. Neufeld), N.Y., Teachers' College Press/London, Cassells, 1993.
4   See, for an overview, Measor, L. and Sikes, P., *Gender and Schools,* London, Cassells, 1992, pp. 109–22.
5   Burgess, R., 'Teacher Careers in a Comprehensive School', in Green, A. and Ball, S. (eds), *Progress and Equality in Comprehensive Education,* London, Routledge, 1988, p. 126.
6   Measor and Sikes, *op. cit.*, p. 115.
7   Benn, C., 'Preface' in DeLyon, H.and Widdowson Migniuolo, F. (eds), *Women Teachers: Issues and Experiences,* Milton Keynes, Open University Press, 1989, p. xix.
8   Board of Education, *Report of the Departmental Committee on the Training of Teachers for Public Elementary Schools,* London, HMSO, 1925, p. 34.
9   See, for example, Burgess, H. and Carter, B., '"Bringing Out the Best In People": Teacher Training and the "Real" Teacher', *British Journal of Sociology of Education* 13, 3, 1992; Steedman, C., 'The Mother Made Conscious: The Historical Development of a Primary School Pedagogy', in Woodhead, M. and McGrath, A. (eds), *Family, School and Society,* Milton Keynes, Open University Press, 1988; Tyler, D., '"Setting the Child Free": Teachers, Mothers and Child-Centered Pedagogy in the 1930's Kindergarten', in Blackmore, J. and Kenway, J. (eds), *Gender Matters in Educational Administration and Policy: A Feminist Introduction*, Falmer, London, 1993; Walkerdine, V., 'Post-Structuralist Theory and Everyday Social Practices: The Family and the School' in Wilkinson, S. (ed.), *Feminist Social Psychology: Development, Theory and Practice,* Milton Keynes, Open University Press, 1986.

10   Central Advisory Council for Education, *Children and Their Primary Schools (The Plowden Report)*, London, HMSO, 1967.

11   Walkerdine, *op. cit.*, p. 59.

12   King, R., *All Things Bright and Beautiful,* Chichester, James Wiley, 1978, p. 72.

13   See for a critical overview, Halpin, D. and Troyna, B. (eds), *Researching Educational Policy: Ethical and Methodological Issues,* London, Falmer, 1994.

14   Plummer, K., *Telling Sexual Stories: Power, Change and Social Worlds,* London, Routledge, 1995, p. 147.

15   Burgess and Carter, *op. cit.*

16   See also Walkerdine, *op. cit.*, p. 58.

17   See Brown, G. and Desforges, C., *Piaget's Theory – A Psychological Critique,* London, Routledge & Kegan Paul, 1979; Cohen, D., *Piaget – Critique and Reassessment,* London, Croom Helm, 1983.

18   See Sikes, P., Measor, L. and Woods, P., *Teacher Careers: Crises and Continuities,* Lewes, Falmer, 1985, pp. 57–69.

19   Grumet, M., *Bitter Milk: Women and Teaching,* Amherst, University of Massachusetts Press, 1988, p. 28

20   Kutnick, P., *Relations in the Primary School Classroom,* London, Paul Chapman, 1988, p. 90.

21   Steedman, C., 'Prisonhouses', in Lawn, M. and Grace, G. (eds), *Teachers: The Culture and Politics of Work,* Lewes, Falmer, 1987.

22   Grumet, *op. cit.*, p. xvi.

23   Cortazzi, M., *Primary Teaching How It Is: A Narrative Account,* London, David Fulton, 1991.

24   Central Advisory Council for Education, *op. cit.*, 167, p. 311.

25   Tyler, *op. cit.*

26   Measor and Sikes, *op. cit.*, p. 41.

27   Walkerdine, V. and Lucey, H., *Democracy in the Kitchen: Regulating Mothers and Socialising Daughters,* London, Virago, 1989, p.178.

28   Cortazzi, *op. cit.*, p. 101–122.

29   For example, Grumet, *op. cit.*; Phoenix, A. and Woollett, A., 'Motherhood: Social Construction, Politics and Psychology', in Phoenix, A., Woollett, A. and Lloyd, E. (eds), *Motherhood: Meanings, Practices and Ideologies,* London, Sage, 1991; Steedman, C., *The Tidy House,* London, Virago, 1982; Walkerdine, *op. cit.*

30   Steedman, *op. cit.*, p. 7.

31   Gitlin, A. and Myers, B., 'Beth's Story: The Search for the Mother Teacher' in McLaughlin, D. and Tierney, W. (eds), *Naming Silenced Lives: Personal Narratives and Processes of Educational Change,* New York, Routledge, 1993, p. 66.

32   Grumet, *op. cit.*, p. 8.

Chapter 5

Telling the Stories
Parents Who Teach

INTRODUCTION

This chapter consists of what I consider to be 'good' stories. They are not 'typical' stories, because I do not believe that there are any, although I know that I could present them as if they were. I chose them because they appealed to me, because I found them interesting, and because I thought that they were illustrative of significant or wider issues than the purely idiosyncratic. It also has to be said that they are the stories of people who had a lot to say and who said it in what was, to me, an entertaining and interesting manner.

I spent a lot of time wondering how to organize the chapter. Should I do it in terms of the type of educational institution the teachers worked in, or by sex or by age? Did I want my organizing principle to be commonalities of experience, or of perspective, and if so which ones? The previous chapters were ordered on these grounds, using the teachers' utterances to substantiate the categories that they and I defined and identified.

I wasn't keen to do this with these life histories, because I felt that by grouping them in a particular way I would be highlighting some things and down-playing others and, thereby, focusing attention in a particular direction. Given that, in terms of this study the key characteristic shared by all of the informants was parenthood, I decided that nothing else was necessary. These stories are, therefore, essentially about teachers' experiences of parenthood. However, it is also the case that they also contribute to the story that I want to tell, and that concerns the ways in which being a parent affects the sort of teacher one is.

Stories about various aspects of parenthood are common. They appear in a range of different published forms, as novels, as 'faction', as factual accounts. They are part of our various cultures: they appear in the Bible, the Q'uran, in Greek and Norse myths and legends, in magazines and newspapers, on the television and in films. People devour them avidly, especially when they describe a difficult situation, a dying child for example, or a parent's fight for the children to live with them rather than with their 'unsuitable' partner. They provide a reassuring function, letting people know that what they are feeling or doing is 'normal' or at least 'good enough'. They educate and provide information. And they offer the people who tell, read, see or hear them an outlet for their worries and concerns. They can give reassurance and may even provide mechanisms for people with similar experiences to make contact with each other. In this respect they work in much the same way as the 'sexual stories' which Ken Plummer talks about.[1]

Generally the 'plot' of the stories revolves around the theme of the 'good' mother or, less commonly, the 'good' parent. What I found interesting about the stories these parent teachers told was the way in which most of them questioned the appropriateness of this concept while still subscribing to it in some way, if only as a flawed notion. Their experiences as parents themselves had led them to challenge the hegemony of the ideal 'good parent' carried in the literature and yet, at the same time, it was the self-same literature which had provided them with a vocabulary and frame of reference for talking about and understanding themselves and others as parents.

Originally my intention was to tell the stories in my own words, using lots of quotes. However, when I came to work on this part of the book I changed my mind and ended up mainly using quotes, interspersed with some commentary which is there in order to provide the necessary contextual information (they are, after all, life histories). In some cases, in Chris's story for instance, there is far more quote than commentary but that is a result of how these particular stories were told. I decided to take this approach because I began to feel that by needlessly changing words and phrases I was distorting what people really wanted to say at the time that they said it. I have, however, and somewhat con-tradictorily, sometimes changed the order of what was said both chronologically, with regard to people's lives and in terms of how it was told to me. This has been done in order to fit, more neatly, into my story. Inevitably there is a danger of misrepresentation but I do not believe that this can ever be avoided. As I noted earlier, stories and, more precisely, life histories, are joint actions and mean nothing on their own. The stories here are simply set within my particular framework. I also know that just as the parent teachers who talked to me might tell their stories differently now than they did at the time when we met, so might I wish to alter mine in six months' or six years' time. But that, as they say, is another story.

TERESA'S STORY

> It just really changes your whole life . . . it's hard to stand back and be objective about the person you are but perhaps, for me, the main thing [about being a parent who is a teacher] is you're less likely to patron-ize children. I am anyway, because you can tell when you're talking to your own children, they're more honest to you about the way you are talking to them. If they don't like the way they've been spoken to they will tell you and so you sort of realize that they're on a different level, but it's not necessarily a lower level to you and you have to remember that they are people, all the time. I think once you've had your own

children it's easier to remember that because there's a constant
reminder at home.

When I talked with Teresa she was aged 22 and was in the fourth and final
year of a BA with Qualified Teacher Status (BAQTS) course. I had been Teresa's
educational studies tutor during her second year and knew her to be a reflective
and critical thinker who expressed her ideas fluently. As she also had a 4-year-
old son, Christopher, who had just started his reception year at school, she was
an ideal informant. Although I was her tutor, Teresa was the senior mother
because, at the time of our conversations, my daughter was eighteen months old
and my son wasn't yet born.

In the section of her book that concerns black women teachers, Kathleen
Casey[2] refers to the power 'problem' involved when whites research aspects of
black people's experience. Casey, who is white, was surprised when her work
was so well received by black academics working in similar fields. They told her
that she 'might have been reading from one of their transcripts'. Hearing this
enabled her to 'finally lay to rest the notion that [her] collection of narratives
had been compromised. What [she] now needed to figure out was why the black
women who produced the life histories were less concerned with (her) racial
identity as (sic) [she] was [herself]'.[3] Casey had thought that her whiteness was
a barrier between her and her black informants. However, she had forgotten or
had not realized that three out of the four women knew that she had a black
daughter. When she remembered she attributed their 'openness' to their knowledge about her daughter and reasoned that they were prepared to talk to her as
if she was herself black. They 'addressed (her) as a person who understood at
least some of the black cultural repertoire, someone who knew some of the pass-
words'.[4]

As I wrote in Chapter 2, although I acknowledge the issues and potential
difficulties involved in understanding and communicating with someone who
has a different life experience and world-view from my own, I do not believe it to
be impossible to do research with them. Teresa was black and a single parent, I
am white and have a husband but I am convinced that this did not 'compromise'
what she told me. Having been one of my students, Teresa was well aware of my
concern about and commitment to equal opportunities, as well as my interest in
biographical and narrative approaches to research. She had, in fact, received
formal and theoretical teaching from me about these subjects so I may even
have contributed to how she conceptualized and talked about the related issues.
We also got on well together and had continued to see each other when she was
no longer in my group. I may be naïve but in my opinion it would be these factors
rather than our different racial backgrounds that had the greatest influence on
how she told me her story and what she included in it. Indeed, she later con-
firmed that this was the case and that also, at the time, what she talked about
were the things which were giving her most concern as a mother and as a
teacher.

Thus it seemed to me that, throughout our talks, Teresa constantly returned to three main themes around the issues of equal opportunities: 'race', social class and single-parenthood. These themes were central to her experiences of life and she talked specifically of how they had influenced her experiences and perceptions as a teacher and as a mother. She told a story concerning her son's self-image which poignantly brought the themes together:

> The school that he's going to isn't multi-cultural in that there aren't many black children. There are a significant number of black children but it doesn't reflect itself, I think, in the policy of the school. I had to complain at one point because all the books that he was bringing home for his reading were two-parent families and they were white. [The class teacher] was a bit touchy about it but I said to her, 'I'm sorry but I just think it needs to be said.' Because all the books that he was bringing home and all the other adults that he was seeing, apart from me and my family, were white, he was getting really confused. So now I think, she's actually given me all the books off the shelf that have a picture of at least one black person in. And there are some brilliant books, I mean there *are* books in the classroom so I couldn't understand why he wasn't bringing them home. OK, there's an element of choice involved in that he's choosing his own books so maybe it's Christopher's choice that's the problem. I actually looked when I went into the classroom and they were all on the shelf behind the others so they weren't going to find them anyway. And then, I think sometimes children choose what they think the teacher wants them to take home, not the book that they actually want. So I thought that there was a problem there. But what I'm doing at home now is, we work together in the evening if we're not too tired because obviously, there are times when we're just so knackered that we just give it a miss, and I really do make an effort to talk to him a lot more now. I think it's really important. I point things out to him in books, or when we're shopping, or on television, when Trevor McDonald [a black newscaster] is on the news and I say, 'Look.' I never used to do that before because I didn't think it was important but I think it's impor- tant for him to have role models of both colours because he's of mixed race, whereas before he was just having one. He used to get really upset about the fact that he was brown, I call myself black, but he's wanted to be, in fact I think he actually thought that he was, white, because he's a lot paler than I am, though he's obviously not as pale as you. And I had to say to him, 'Well, you know people are going to see you as brown or black, no matter how you see yourself. You might think that you're white but you're actually not because you come from mummy and your daddy was white.' I had to go through this whole thing, even though he was only 4 and the poor little thing was proba-

bly completely confused. But now he just accepts it so it obviously worked, over a period of time. And he says now, 'I'm brown and you're black and nanny's black' and we have to go through this rigmarole. But I think that it's important for him to just accept the colour that he is because you can't bring up a child as something that they're not, no matter how comfortable they might seem in it at the time, it's going to get harder and harder to do that. I know someone who brought up her son as white, or the fact that he was black wasn't an issue because he was of mixed race as well, and he's really confused now because he's 14 and some of his friends are white and some are black and other people obviously see him as black but he can't understand this because his mother's white. And it's hard for him now and I don't want Christopher to go through that. Even though I think you can labour the point sometimes, it's not being addressed at school so I think I need to do it at home. I don't think that I'd have had the awareness to do that if I hadn't come here [on a teacher education course]. Little things like that I possibly wouldn't have thought about, I'd just have left them and they would probably fester and get worse as he got older so I'm sorting them out now because I think it's really important for him.

Although Teresa believed that Christopher's teacher possessed inherent qualities which made her 'brilliant' with reception-age children, she thought that she was insufficiently aware of Chris's needs as a black child. Teresa was also concerned about the teacher's views on single-parent families which, she had heard, stemmed from the woman's Christian beliefs. The school in question had an intake that was mainly working class and Teresa felt that the teacher's values might be out of place in such a setting.

What had happened was, I bought some gloves and they had cardboard cut-outs of hands in them and I said 'Well, you can colour them in', and he coloured them in pink. And I was a bit surprised and I said 'Well, why did you colour them in pink Christopher?' And he said, 'Well, everybody's hands are pink aren't they?' And I honestly thought that he meant the palms which is fair enough and I would have left it but I said 'Well, look at your hands' and he said 'Oh yes', and he coloured them in black. And I thought, he's going to be really confused but I was really shocked and I hadn't explained why to the teacher, but we're supposed to have a meeting soon and I think I will then because I think she needs to know why. I was so upset. . . . I was talking to another education tutor and he said, 'Well, you should have done it, even though you might have upset her. It needs to be said and maybe she needs to be upset because sometimes it's the only way to get anything done is to upset people.' She's about 40 and she's a committed Christian, apparently, and she's got very strong views on family life. My childminder told me that. And I said 'Well, that's her thing.' If she wants to have that outside the classroom that's fair enough but she can't bring those values into school with her. She has to leave them at the door and just get on with the way things are in the classroom. Because it's a very working-class area anyway and there are going to be lots of single-parent families there so she's just going to have to accept the idea that that's the way that it is. And I don't think she has, in her own mind yet. Which is why Chris is coming in and that's why all his books were the way they were. And she did say as well that the problem with having more multi-cultural books and books that involve single-parent families was money. But there are some there, in the classroom. So she obviously has them but she's not using them.

Having had a professional teacher education, Teresa felt that she was both equipped to make an interpretation of what was going on in her son's classroom and sufficiently confident to talk to his teacher about it. She spoke therefore, as a mother who was a teacher.

I'm definitely a lot more – awful jargon word – proactive than I would have been if I hadn't been a teacher, well, student teacher. If I hadn't been I definitely wouldn't have spoken to the teacher about it, definitely wouldn't.

Out of necessity Teresa had done all of her school practices in the 'working-class' schools close to the university creche attended by her son. What she had observed led her to the opinion that,

In working-class schools the children just aren't encouraged enough by the teachers, not just at home. It's all very well for the teachers to say, 'Well, they're not encouraged to read at home you know. They watch telly all the time.' There's a sort of laziness on the part of a lot of the teachers which, they'll say, 'Well, they're working class anyway. They're never going to get very far in life so why should we be bothered?' I think it's important to make them see that they can. I got somewhere. I went to working-class schools and I'm here now, so if I can do it, they can as well. Although it's important to remember that not every child has got the potential to get to university but they've still got potential. And not everybody wants to get to university either.

Teresa's own school experiences had been good. Like many people she had memories of a special teacher who had been very significant and who had had some influence on her own choice of career:

I started school in London and it was a very multi-cultural area.
There were very few white kids in the school that I started in and
there just wasn't a problem because the white teachers were as into
multi-cultural education as the black ones, so there wasn't any problem there. And I actually learnt to read really quickly because I was
encouraged such a lot that by the end of the first term I could read
while at the beginning I couldn't, because I was really lazy. My mum
tried before I started school and I just couldn't be bothered. And I had
a white teacher who really encouraged me, took me to the library in
town, took me out of school and got me to join the library. And she was
brilliant. I think, if it hadn't been for her I probably wouldn't be here
now because I just wouldn't have any interest in school at all because
most of the kids just couldn't be bothered. But if she saw any potential
in any child, black or white, she'd really try and encourage it. Which is
what I think the role of a teacher is, rather than trying to get kids to
be what you want them to be, it's to try and get them to be as good as
they can be.

Mairtin Mac an Ghaill has described how, in some schools, some black students show their rejection of 'school values' by developing a culture in which
conformity is seen as a form of race disloyalty or treachery.[5] A similar thing can
happen with regard to class. Teresa had experienced this.

At my next primary school they were just as good as they had been in
London. I was encouraged a lot there as well, although it was harder
there because you tended to get bullied if you worked hard, especially
if you were black. I was actually bullied by another black boy. He must
have thought I was a real traitor because I was in with these white
people who were working hard and I think it was difficult for him to
accept.

Although she was not bullied at her secondary school, Teresa was aware of
the strength of the anti-school culture and of how black and working-class
pupils are expected to subscribe to it. She, however, continued to work hard, to
her teachers' surprise:

I was really lucky in the secondary school. I went round with a group
of black girls, there were a few white girls as well, and they just
weren't interested in school at all but they didn't mind the fact that I
was. And I still see them now and it was really nice because it was
almost like a protection thing. They didn't mind that I was good. It
really is unusual. Looking back, a teacher of mine that I used to have,
he said he was so surprised that I actually got any O-levels. I got nine,
and he was really surprised because he thought, going around with

them I probably wouldn't have any interest in school. He said it was wrong of him to assume that, but looking back he could understand why he did. I mean, they used to smoke and they never pressurized me into doing anything that I didn't want to do and yet we were all really good friends. And I can't understand why we were myself, looking back. It stopped me from being a snob. They encouraged me but they never let me get above themselves.

Teresa had always thought that she might like to teach so when she was in the sixth form she took up an opportunity to teach younger pupils with reading difficulties. She enjoyed this and subsequently applied for and obtained a place on, a teacher education course at a college in London. However, before the end of her final year at school she found out that she was pregnant, decided that she wanted to have her baby, and gave up her place.

I gave up my place because I didn't want to move to London on my own with a baby. It would be too expensive with no sort of family support, which I knew I was going to need. So I knew I was going to stay here [at least for the next few years].

After her son was born, Teresa's intention was still to go on to higher education but at a local university this time:

After I had Christopher I went back to [my secondary school] and asked if I could help with the children with special needs in the first- and second-year classes. I knew I didn't want to work in secondary school but I thought, I know the staff here, they'll help me out, they'll give me tips . . . so for a year I did this. . . . I'd lost a lot of confidence between leaving school and having Chris and I thought that if I don't do this I'm not going to have the confidence to apply for university.

Conscious of the way in which teaching is seen as a job that is both suitable for mothers and also for people who lack qualifications to do other things, Teresa took action:

I didn't want it to be something that I did just because I had a baby so I applied for another degree course, sociology and education, and I got a place. But I also went for the BAQTS course because that was what I really wanted to do. If I'd done the joint degree I'd have still done a PGCE but I really wanted to teach. I just didn't want people to think that it was the only thing I could do.

Other people's perceptions of how 'good' mothers should behave, in particular the understanding that 'good' mothers do not go out to work, had touched Teresa.

I really resent people thinking that because I've got a child there's
only so much I can do. And I know there are people here who think
that I shouldn't be here. And I'm not just talking about older people,
I'm talking about students who are younger than me as well, who
think I should be at home. . . . There are a lot of students here who
think I should be being a 'mum' and that I'm not a good parent
because I'm here and he goes to a childminder and Chris was in the
creche and these little things. I think younger students tend to be
more bigoted than older ones because older ones have got the experience of life behind them to know that you can't be narrow-minded. . . .
[A group of us who have our own children] were talking the other day
and we actually said it was really depressing that most of the people
we know on this course we wouldn't want teaching our own children.
. . . I would feel really uncomfortable about most of the people on the
infant variant teaching Christopher. I just wouldn't be happy about it
at all.

It is significant that the students she is referring to will, one day, become teachers and will have an influence, through their beliefs, on the children that they
teach. Perhaps if they have their own children they will revise some of their
opinions as so many of the parent teachers I talked with claimed to have done.
Teresa, however, was concerned to offer an alternative picture, right from the
start. It was clear that her experiences as a mother, and, in particular as a
single parent, would affect her attitude to teaching, her experience of it, her
pedagogy, what she taught and where she taught as well:

As a single-parent teacher I think I'm more broadminded. I think
when you're 17 you have things like you're going to get married and
you're going to have a family and 2.7 kids and a dog and a house and
two cars and this. Life happens and you realize it's not like that at all
and I think I'm more prepared now to accept exceptions to the rule in
the classroom. . . . I want to teach in areas where I won't feel that my
family situation is abnormal and I won't transfer that onto the children because it's just not going to work if I'm made to feel all the time
that the way we live isn't right. I remember on my last practice, I
don't usually tell them anything about my private life but a little girl
asked me if I'd got kids and, I'm always honest, I said yes. And she
said 'You're *Miss* D, you're not married.' And I said, 'Well, some people
don't get married before they have children and there are people who
get married and have children and then aren't married anymore', and
she thought about it and she said yes, and she thought about children
in the class who came from single-parent families and she accepted it
then. But it's something that you have to remind people about, that
we do exist and we are functioning and we aren't all on social security

and we aren't all drug addicts. People tend to assume that you must
have all these problems going on in your life if you're a single parent.

Teresa's story has to be interpreted in the light of her experiences of being a
black single parent living in a racist society. Her feeling was that because she
was identified in these terms she had to continually and consciously take certain actions in order to avoid meeting other people's expectations of what she
was likely to, could and should do. In contradiction to these expectations she has
been academically successful. She attributes this largely to being 'fortunate'
with regard to some of the teachers she came into contact with, and in her
friends at secondary school who did not pressurize her to conform with their
anti-school attitude.

Then there is Teresa as a young, black single mother. Such mothers have an
image of being feckless, dependent upon state benefit and possibly drug-users
as well. Teresa was concerned to mount a public challenge to this stereotype for
the sake of her own son and for other children too. As a teacher she felt that she
was in a position to educate by offering an alternative picture to the one which
dominates public consciousness. Her motivation to do this was given urgency
because of her love for, and desire to protect, Christopher.

As a mother, she felt that her concerns about racism were given an added
edge. She knew that things would be difficult for her son as a direct result of his
colour. Drawing on her own experience as a black woman in a white male-
dominated society, on her professional knowledge, and on what she had learnt in
the course of her academic and theoretical study of racism and sexism, she
embarked on a specific programme of work with, and on behalf of, the boy. Her
intention is to provide him with what he needs in order to be himself, rather
than 'a mixed race child from a single-parent family'. Once again this work will
spill over into what she does in school. So, for example, Teresa will try to make
sure that the black children she may teach in the future do not make the confused assumption that they have white hands. In doing this she will be acting in
the capacity of what Braxton, cited in Casey,[6] describes as the 'outraged mother'
who protects her own and all other black children, from the depredations of
racism.

Teresa is conscious that some black people regard her as a 'race traitor' who
has 'sold out' to white culture. She has, after all, become a teacher and, therefore, might reasonably be expected to be in the business of maintaining the
status quo. She doesn't, however, see things in this way herself. For a start she
was interested in and enjoyed learning for its own sake and had felt that she
needed to study in order to understand what was going on with regard to racism
and equal opportunities more generally. Casey suggests that black people who
succeed within the white education system 'refute its (re)production of black
inferiority materially and symbolically'.[7] Furthermore, the black women she
talked to did not 'see themselves as *individuals* striving for academic achievement; within the institutions of education they are interpellated as, and choose

to present themselves as, representatives *of* and *for* their people'.[8] These were Teresa's feelings too but it is important to remember that they were intertwined with, and strengthened by, her perceptions and experiences as a black mother teacher. With this emphasis in mind it is significant that she intended to leave teaching when her son was a bit older and when she felt more financially secure. To some extent she was being a teacher because she was a mother, because teaching provided her with the practical necessities of money and 'convenient hours' which she particularly needed as a single parent. In addition though, she did feel a sense of mission to make things better for her son and also for other children. For Teresa, therefore, being a teacher was inextricably bound up with being a mother, and being a mother made her the sort of teacher that she saw herself as being.

KAREN'S STORY

> [Being a mother who's a teacher] has had a sort of negative effect really, with my own children. And I desperately tried not to say it to them but I found myself sometimes thinking if they're complaining, or if they're moaning, or if I've been dealing with some children with desperate needs then I feel like saying, 'For God's sake! You don't know how lucky you are.' And I thought, no, you mustn't do that because they need to have a valve for moaning really. But it does do that to you. You think, my kids shouldn't moan at all really. They have it easy. So it might make you a little less sympathetic towards your own children in a funny way.

When I went to see Karen, who I knew through a mutual friend, one of the first things she said was that since she'd agreed to take part in the research, she'd been thinking about what it had been like for her children to have a parent who was a teacher. At the time when we spoke her son was 16 and her daughter was 18. This meant that she was able to look back over most of their school careers and, although there had been benefits, she had come to the conclusion that, for a number of reasons, some things had been quite difficult for them as a result of her job. For instance although she had tried to avoid doing it, she had, on occasion, compared them with the children she taught and came into contact with at school. Regardless of the nature of the comparison, or of whether they came out 'better' or 'worse', she thought that this had been an irritating and uncomfortable experience which could have had quite seriously negative effects both in terms of her relationship with them and for their own self-perception. She knew that there had been times when they had felt that other people got more of her than they did, even though she had always been acutely conscious of their needs and had tried to be there for them. She recognized that, to a large extent, the demands on her time now were due to her being a head teacher. However, because her work had always involved other children there had been more scope and greater grounds for resentment than there would have been had she worked in a bank for example. Somewhat ironically though, she was aware that the teachers her children got on well with were themselves parents.

> Thinking about my own children at secondary school, the teachers that they relate to are the ones that they would go to if they had problems, I'm sure that, on the whole, they are the ones who've got, particularly, teenage children. Because I know one in particular who helped Lucy, had. She really understood what was going on because teenage years are horrendous.

Not surprisingly teachers' children tend to have a more 'realistic' view of teachers as 'ordinary' people than others do and Karen believed that, in her son's case, this had led to him getting into trouble at school.

> They know about teachers because they're at home. Not just their parents but their parents' friends as well. They know they're just ordinary people, there isn't that mystique.

Then there is the professional knowledge that teachers possess which might lead to them making extra demands on their children, or regulating their activities more closely. On reflection Karen felt that she had, perhaps, been rather too 'correct' with her children as a result of what she had learnt at college and from the parenting books:

> You are more aware of the developmental stages and things and the sorts of toys, I suppose, educational-type toys. I look back now and I think perhaps I did too much of that. Perhaps I should have bought them more crap. I can remember L desperately wanting a Sindy doll, and me saying, 'Well, if you want a Sindy you'll have to buy one.' And she did. She saved up her money and bought herself one. And I look back now and I think if I had children now I'd be a lot more laid back about it. I was into 'You must do the *right* thing' and I think it was all this stuff from college about Plowden. I think I'd be a lot more relaxed about it. I was a bit uptight about it all I suppose, really. I wasn't so much with the second. I was particularly with the first child but I wouldn't buy guns, and then you found them making them, though they'd say 'No, it's not a gun', pretending it wasn't. I suppose no one's an ideal parent. . . . If you're not relaxed as a parent, if you're doing something because you think you have to do it and you don't actually feel right doing it, are you actually doing your child any favours? I do think there is a change and that we're actually coming away from the experts telling us what to do. It's about women taking control.

Listening to this I could have been hearing myself talking about my own abortive struggles for 'political correctness' with Robyn and Joby. In our case, Robyn managed to buy a longed-for Barbie doll for a pound from a car boot sale, proving herself a successful bargainer as much as anything else, while Joby had fashioned himself a 'shooter' from a soft toy snake. In other ways too, Karen's story was very similar to my own. This was probably because we were of similar age, she was 42 and I was 39, and we both came from working-class homes and got into teaching for similar reasons and by similar routes:

> How did I come into teaching? It was really boring! I was greatly influenced by my own reception-class teacher, if I look back. I was desperate to go to school as a child. Loved it when I got there and wanted to be a teacher and very boringly, that's what I became. Awful, isn't it! So I went from school to college to school which, on reflection now, I think was a big mistake. I think I should at least have had a year out to do something else because I now feel that sort of, what else can I do? . . . It was to do with my home background I think. No one in my family had ever gone on to the sixth form or anything, let alone on to further or higher education, and I don't think I even thought about doing anything else. Nobody advised me about anything. My parents didn't really know anything about going on to college or anything, so I just did it. . . . So, from a small, very rural village in Devon, I moved to the bright lights of a midlands city and to a place on a three-year teaching certificate course. . . . While I was at college I got married. . . . I was in the second year, and I met and married P within three months, much to my parents' horror and everybody else's horror. I mean I hadn't intended to come to college here and stay, but I did.

Karen was lucky in her first job in that she found herself working with like-minded colleagues who were, albeit for unfortunate reasons, a united group.

> I saw teaching as building a relationship with the children and obviously there was the reading and writing, the basic skills, but also developing them as people. For them to look at how they related to people. I was in a school and out of the six of us [teaching there] I think five of us have become head teachers who were there in the year that I went. It was quite a dynamic sort of staff. I did three years there and I found that it really helped me. We were in a school where everybody didn't think much of the head so there was this united feeling among the staff and I learnt a lot from colleagues.

In 1976, two years after she started work, Karen had her first child:

> Having kids was just something I took for granted. I'd been married
> for three or four years and we did want children.

She took the minimum maternity leave which, at the time, was seventeen weeks, eleven before and six after the birth, and went back to work leaving her husband at home to look after the baby.

> It was for practical reaons. P. was in a job that wasn't particularly
> secure. He was working in a warehouse and it just seemed, I mean
> there was no great sort of political reason for me going back to work or
> anything, but it was just the most practical thing to do.

When her second child was born, three years later, maternity leave was a much more generous seven months (although this was not all at full pay) which made things considerably easier.

Despite having her husband at home, Karen still felt that she needed to be a 'proper' mum. Eventually, however, she was able to get rid of the guilt that is felt by many working mothers, but much more rarely by fathers:

> When I first had my own children and I was at work I used to get home
> and think I've now got to do all these things with them. But I think
> what helped was that I went on a women teachers' course. I ended up
> running them eventually, but it was run by the union. It was really
> about looking at guilt, you know, assertiveness, all that. And if I look
> back that was a very significant bit. I came away from that with all
> sorts of new things but actually thinking, 'You can't be superwoman.
> I've got to stop feeling guilty. This is an impossible thing I'm trying to
> do. Get rid of the guilt and just concentrate on what you can do'. And I
> don't feel guilty about the children and being a working mother at all.
> I actually think they've gained from it and become more independent.

Having had her own children Karen started to see her pupils in a rather different light:

> I suppose I started to see the children more in the context of their
> family than just pupils in school . . . actually thinking about them out-
> side of school as well.

By the time that I talked with her, Karen was the head of a thriving community primary school which served a predominantly Asian population. She was well known locally through her work in the school, within the LEA, at the university where she sat on the teacher training advisory panel, and by her involvement in union activities. She also had something of a national reputation because she had written articles for journals about work that had been done at her school, and because the school had participated in various projects that had been widely reported. Despite, or because of, these extra activities and interests, Karen was firmly committed to her school and the families which it served.

As a head, Karen's views on what made a 'good' teacher were significant because they influenced who she appointed to work in her school. For her a 'good' teacher was,

> someone who can form good and vital relationships with everybody, with children and the other adults in school, I think. If you've got someone who finds it hard to relate to children, you're on a loser really. Someone who understands how children learn . . . I think the National Curriculum has pushed people to thinking children learn in sort of sequential steps. Someone who can deal with individual children's needs as well as seeing the class as a whole. It is a sort of empathy thing, I think, which comes into the relationships about understanding. Being a parent helps. Having your own children doesn't necessarily mean you're a good teacher but it gives you a good start. You might not be a very good parent either!

Like everyone else I talked with, Karen felt that one of the most important ways in which she had changed since having her own children was in how she regarded other parents. She found that she had become much less ready to 'pass judgement' on the way in which people lived their lives, and she was concerned that the staff at her school should adopt the same approach:

> One thing we say here is we try not to make value judgements about people's lifestyles. And we had quite a long discussion as a staff for a while about that. Even if we don't come originally from middle-class families we are living middle-class lives now and we can't assume that our lifestyle is the right one and then think everybody else has got to aim to be like us. And I think that's quite hard for a lot of people.

One reason why it can be hard is because people lack basic information about other ways of living. However, Karen's school had been involved in a national project on education for parenthood. As part of this, parents had been invited into school to join in workshops dealing with parenting practices and values. As most of these parents came from a different cultural tradition there had been a considerable amount of learning on each side. Consequently teachers had been able to take from this and match their teaching to the needs of their pupils more appropriately. This served to further emphasise the links between parenting and teaching.

When Karen's son got into trouble at his school and she was the mother being summoned to a meeting, rather than the head teacher calling it, she felt even more empathy with parents. While she found the whole experience extremely upsetting, she was also able to make use of it, not only insofar as it allowed her to share common ground and establish rapport with parents she had to speak to about their 'naughty' children, but also because it helped her to devise more sensitive ways of contacting and talking with them.

The majority of the pupils at Karen's school came from relatively poor, although caring, homes. In addition, their parents were often not fluent or literate in English. These factors, coupled with Karen's experiences of having to help her own children with school work, affected how she organized such things as parents' meetings and the school's policy on children taking work home. In their research into mothers' involvement in home/school links, David, Edwards, Hughes and Ribbens found that 'the implications for family life of (homework) are generally left unremarked, since all parents are expected to support the school defined educational endeavours without comment'.[9] Karen took a more empathetic view:

> We have a lot of parents who say, 'I feel really awful because I can't
> read English and I can't speak English.' We do very much think that
> the most important thing is to show an interest, even just to talk to
> them about what they've done at school today or to share a book. When
> we have open evenings here we get nearly 100 per cent attendance,
> and that speaks volumes. There is an interest there and we use those
> times to talk to parents who say, 'Well, what can I do?' We don't have
> homework, we have some pressure from people to give homework but
> we actually feel that we don't want to be sending children home with
> work to do which is then a pressure on the family. A lot of our children
> live in quite crowded accommodation. And parents are up to their eyes
> in it, you know, lots of children or mothers are working at home, doing
> sewing, or they're out to work. We don't actually push that. I actually
> know what it's like. My children used to come home with things and I'd
> think Oh! Bloody hell! The reality of most of our families is that they
> are very, very busy. Often living in very stressful situations where the
> last thing on their mind would be 'Come along dear. Do this, do that.' I
> chose not to get involved in a particular maths project because it relied
> on kids taking work home. They don't need it.

Karen was conscious that organizational decisions such as not to give homework or not to have a school uniform could have negative implications.

> You see, now we're into this competitive thing. This is really starting
> to rear its head now. It's been particularly so with the local authority
> looking to remove surplus places.

She felt that the pressure was on to compete with other schools to attract children and she knew that parents often looked to the obvious and visible signs which, they believed, identified 'good' schools. Karen, however, was adamant that the emphasis on caring and accommodation which extended into the local community and which characterized her school was more important than uniforms and homework could ever be. She worried about the future.

> This is what worries me about teacher training now. I don't feel there's going to be that theoretical base, that at the time you may not feel is particularly useful but you refer back to it. . . . I worry about the teachers of the future . . . and I worry about what definitions of a 'good' teacher are being used. If you're looking at it very narrowly in a sort of academic way. You see the government perspective on a teacher now, they would disregard all this. Their view is that you're there to progress the children academically and that's it.

In conventional terms Karen has had an extremely successful career. She has got to 'the top' and has also been involved in a variety of activities outside her immediate job. The pattern of her working life has, therefore, been more like that of a man than of a woman. This impression is heightened by the fact that her husband took on the child-care role more usually filled by a woman. Who can tell the extent to which this contributed to her success, but the decision to focus, initially, on her career rather than Peter's inevitably helped. Taking time out on maternity leave is widely regarded as a reason why women are not as successful in the promotion stakes as men are. The evidence suggests, however, that the assumptions that those responsible for appointments have about mother teachers' commitment, play a far greater part than the actual amount of time that women take off when they do have children.[10]

Karen's children were born in the late 1970s when provision for maternity leave was even less generous than it had come to be by the time of writing. Expectations that mothers would be 'proper', stay-at-home mums with total responsibility for child care were also, perhaps, stronger. Consequently Karen and Peter's 'role reversal' did not come easily. Until she worked out her 'guilt', 'guilt' which I think is still felt by the vast majority of working mothers today, Karen felt that she needed to try and be as much like a full-time mum as possible, regardless of the fact that she also worked full time. She couldn't easily jetison what was expected of her as a 'good' mother, especially when the expectations were those of her children who were comparing her with their friends' stay-at-home mums. As a result of this, when she became a head teacher, her personal and acute consciousness of how working parents and their children can feel when they aren't able to attend daytime school activities led her to make organizational arrangements that differ from what is usual. The fundamental difference lay in the way in which times and dates for parents to come into school were not based on taken-for-granted, hegemonic assumptions about how families work but rather took account of what really happened in her pupils' homes.

Like Teresa, Karen was driven by a commitment to equality of opportunity.

This had influenced both where she worked, what she did, and the amount of time that she put into her job. However, whereas Teresa was partly motivated by a desire to make things better for her son, Karen felt that her own children were especially lucky, materially, emotionally and intellectually, and she wanted to improve the opportunities open to others.

In some respects Karen was fortunate in that she went to college and started work at a particular time when her values and what she wanted to do within education were not in opposition to official policy. Although she came from a working-class background which made actually finding her way into higher education not that easy, she went to college at a time when student grants were sufficient to live on. She received a liberal professional education in which the main emphasis was on child-centred learning and the development of the full potential of each individual child. While she now saw some problems with certain of the things she had been taught, she was still fundamentally committed to such an approach, both as a teacher and as a mother. As a result of this she was unhappy with the shift to a more standardized and instrumental approach to education that characterized the right-wing 'reforms' of the 1980s and 1990s. She was also concerned about the effect that the official propagation of social values concerning such things as families and 'morality' could have upon children living in circumstances which did not match those being recommended. Like many teachers of her generation Karen was depressed about the way that schools and schooling appeared to her to be going and also about the implications for her own children and the children she taught. As a teacher and as a mother concerned about children's development the future looked somewhat grim but she continued to be motivated by the idea that 'her bit' mattered and was worth doing.

CHRIS'S STORY

I first met Chris twelve and a half years ago when I did some life history work with him for a project focusing on teachers' lives and careers.[11] At that time we had spent around twelve hours talking together and I felt that I had got to know him quite well. He was one of the easiest people I have ever done this kind of work with: he spoke easily, with little prompting, although I never got the impression that he was reciting a well-rehearsed script. He said, and I believed him, that he was glad of the opportunity to reflect out loud because it helped him sort his thoughts out. I was certainly pleased to have such a fluent and reflective key informant.

As is usually the case, when the teacher careers project ended, we lost touch, although, like all the other people I had interviewed for it, he was regularly brought to mind when I gave lectures and talks on life history. I had also thought about him when I started my research on parenthood and teaching because on our last meeting Chris had told me that he just learnt that he was to become a father and this news had made him more interested in promotion than he previously had been.

> As soon as I heard my wife was pregnant I thought 'Oh! Money!' Mainly because my wife's working now . . . but she won't be able to do that after a couple more months so it's going to be pressure, moneywise, so I've got to think about that. . . . So I am looking for a Scale 2.[12]

Prior to this Chris's ambitions had been only partly within the school system. At the time he was 28 and was working as an art teacher in a secondary school in a very difficult area of a northern city. He did not intend to stay there for ever, or even for very much longer:

> I am now wanting to get – still with an element of teaching but being able to carry on with things – personal, individual work of my own, at the same time. My ideal is to get a job part-time teaching in an art college – like it is for most other art teachers.[13]

When I learnt, quite by accident and twelve years on, that Chris was still in the same city but working as member of the art department in a different school, I wondered what had happened in the intervening years. I was interested in following up his experiences of parenthood so I decided to write to him and ask if he would agree to talk with me again. Luckily he did and we arranged to meet.

I went along at the appointed time feeling slightly apprehensive. The last time we had met he was 28 and I was 27 and we were both at the start of our careers. Now we were 40 and 39 respectively. A lot of things I had never even imagined had happened to me over the last twelve years and I assumed it had been the same for him. For a start, and pertinently, I had two children that I had never expected to have and he had three, two sons aged 11 and 10 and a 4-year-old daughter. It was strange, but when he came into the room it was almost as if we had only been talking to each other the previous week. I think this was due partly to the type of people we both are but also to the nature of the relationship we had established so long ago. Life history work is, after all, concerned with getting to know people, so we did share quite a lot of intimate and significant information about each other. This enabled us to more or less pick up where we had left off.

Once again Chris proved to be a considered and fluent speaker. And once again he told me that he welcomed the opportunity to review aspects of his life:

> I thought it'd be nice to come and talk to you because more and more I'm getting into more thinking about things, rather than doing things all the time, whereas I was a more practical-based person before and I did things all the time. I thought that was the way but, it's probably partly getting old, you tend to start contemplating things more and

consider your situation, especially when you get to 40. As that time comes everyone seems to assess their situation, in everything, working, family and everything. I don't know why. It seems to be half way or something like that. People pressurize you to think as well, at that time. Everybody says everybody's changing their lifestyle, now you've got to be thinking about 'Oh, is this how you want it for ever?' And it does make you think. I've been considering things a lot more than I used to do. I haven't done any art for the last few months but I still do produce things. Yes, the opportunity to review things is quite in my mind now so I don't mind this.

It is interesting that what Chris says fits neatly into the male life-cycle models proposed by psychologists such as Erickson,[14] Jung[15] and Levinson et al.[16] Back in my days on the teachers' careers project I had made considerable use of such models in analysing the life histories of the teachers we talked to. I had written that,

There is considerable evidence which suggests that between the approximate ages of thirty-seven to forty-five individuals experience a phase which can be at least as traumatic as adolescence. . . . Crucially it is during this phase that it becomes apparent whether or not the work of establishing occupational career, family and identity, begun in the twenties and thirties has been successful; and it tends to involve self-reappraisal, questioning what one has made of one's life and searching for ways of expressing, fulfilling and satisfying oneself in the future. It is the transitional phase from youth to maturity and . . . the central issue is coming to terms with one's own mortality.[17]

Chris's reappraisal focused on the relationship between his marriage, his children and his work:

I've just been off for a week because we've had a lot of trouble at home. That might not be relevant to what you're going to find out but it probably will be because it's all connected, kids and things and work and everything like that. So I've done more thinking in the last six months than I've ever done in my life and work's taken something of a back seat.

To some extent, Chris attributed his 'trouble' to the way in which he had treated his family, and his eldest son in particular, as a consequence of working at the school where I had first met him. He had moved from that school to his present one five years ago when the opportunity to be redeployed had arisen. This new school was in a much more socially advantaged area of the city.

I fancied a change anyway and that was my first school and it's not considered healthy to stay in one school all that time. And it probably wasn't, but you don't know unless you swap round schools. And it does you good to see other ways of working and different approaches with different kids. The effect that — school had on my life was quite striking you know, the way I treated my kids as a result of being there that I wasn't aware of until I left.

Of course, things are rarely quite so straightforward and Chris acknowledged this. He did, however, feel certain that his eldest son had suffered as a result of his inexperience as a parent and because he had worked in a specifically difficult environment where the majority of the children came from what was described by the head teacher as an 'underclass' area. Lacking familiarity with kids, Chris had taken what he did at school as a model and had applied it at home, with distressing consequences.

The eldest is hard work and the other two aren't. The first one was always tricky. . . . I often think, has he turned out a certain way because he was the first child, and we just didn't know how to treat kids in the appropriate way – it was a trial sort of thing. And we found out we shouldn't have done that, but it was done anyway. That's why he's a bit stroppy. And the other two, we got it about right. By the third one, because it was a girl, we thought, marvellous, we can do it now! It was all very easy then. But I don't think it's that really. But the effect of — school, the way that I had to react to the pupils there, because I thought that was the way, was a very aggressive way. And I didn't realize until it was drummed into me when I got home, that I was doing it when I got home, and I'd got absolutely nothing left for my own kids, well, own kid, then. And I used to shout at him as soon as I walked in the door. Well, he was probably doing something wrong but the effect of me picking on something that he'd done wrong, was not very good at all. So he ended up not liking me very much for quite a while. But you don't realize that. I was just treating him like a pupil. You know, when something was wrong you tell them and you shout at them. Whereas at home you should just ignore little things because they don't matter. You're with them all night and all day and you can get over it and not jump on them. Although the same offence committed half an hour earlier at school you'd have to jump on. It was that sort of change that I wasn't aware of. But you were with your own children and you had to treat them in a different way. I thought you treat children all the same and they'll all behave the same but they want different things, don't they, and they expect different things and you can't be a teacher with your own. It took a long time to get out of the feeling like a teacher when I got home. Very often you don't until the holidays, two weeks into the holidays you realize that you're a human again and not a teacher. I mean it takes that long sometimes. At — school it used to take longer because you felt terrible the first week and the second you'd start to be feeling all right. But at my present school you're not as wound up at the end of the day so you can be calm when you get home and don't have to sit down and mentally switch off before you go and talk to people. At — school you had to have a break and do something that took your mind off it, because you were dealing with all their problems and you couldn't carry them home too much because they weren't your responsibility. But it was only my wife that pointed out that I was being like this and I didn't know. I'm quite aware that how other people see you is different. You know how you feel yourself but you don't know what you look like to someone who only sees you when you come home for five minutes before they go out to play. You know, that's the image they retain, of you pointing out what they've done wrong straight away, as soon as you see them. I mean we had to go to a psychologist with the eldest one because we thought he had behavioural problems. I now think he doesn't. I think he's just very sensitive and picks things up. He's very insecure really and his insecurity comes out in terms of hiding it by being naughty. He's very worried about things. I don't know where he's got that from. He might have got it from his parents, I don't know. But being able to look at yourself and stand back from yourself a little bit, you couldn't, you didn't have time to at — school. You were too tired. But here, it does allow you to do that a little bit. It's just as well. You start to lose touch with your family completely.

As well as being concerned about how he was behaving towards the boy, Chris wondered, as Karen had with regard to her son, whether simple familiarity with teachers was at the root of the problem.

He was causing trouble at school and being rude at home and shouting and everything. And I thought, it's because I'm a teacher he's being bad at school because he thinks you can do anything you want with them because your dad's one. They're nothing. It took me a long time to think is that it? . . . as I say we saw a psychologist . . . and we got absolutely nowhere really because there wasn't a real problem like that. You want people to step in sometimes and just stand back and say, 'Oh try this.' Very often it's something very simple and you do the same sort of thing with kids at school, you think about ways of treating them differently but you very often ignore what you're doing at home.

As is the case for most people, although perhaps particularly for women, having children had dramatically changed Chris's and his wife's lives. When we talked, their marriage was under stress, partly because of the children and because, again like most other people, they had not fully appreciated the consequences of having them. These problems had led to him thinking about where work fitted into the whole picture:

> I can't say I liked children particularly you know, then [when we first talked]. It was something you don't know about. I'm sure I said then there was a fear of the unknown. [He did!] For a long time they were hard work, they were very hard work because everything you'd done before had to change, as I thought it would, But I couldn't imagine at the beginning how I could possibly live like that, staying up all night, then getting up for work, then going again, then coming back, cooking the tea. Because my wife found it very hard to start with and I had to help a lot to begin with. But she couldn't cope very well with the night time bit so I had to be getting up all night with one of them. It's difficult, as you know, when you're doing that all of the time. But then unfortunately another one of them came along the next year. Apparently they say that the gap between them is not good if you get like 18 months between them it just doesn't help at all. You've got to get more of a gap because there's one just still in nappies and still mucking about and the other one's just come along then and they grow up with this sort of space between them and it's not very helpful. They're close, but not very close and so there's never one that can look after the other, there's never the sort of an age difference to be useful to you. We should have had the spacing a bit better but you can't plan everything can you? But fortunately the last one was better because the other two can look after her a bit, which is an advantage. Having three you think, three's all right. It's just like two with another one, but three's something else. Because we initially thought three kids wouldn't be a problem. We could cope with it, make room for them, and everything. And you do but it takes something from you because you have to give a lot. The thing it took from us was just having time to ourselves all the time. We had to give up thinking about ourselves for quite a number of years. . . . We've had to start thinking about it because we've been through hell in the last few months. But that was because we've got older and changed but we don't know each other any more and we'll have to try and find that. 'What on earth did we get married for?' and sort of things like that, basic things. It was only through going through that that you realize what you think about your own kids. What it'd be like if you didn't have them any more. You know, can you consider that? Then I thought, in relation to work, you think, well, what on earth are you working for? You're working

because it's fun? Well, bits of it are but I could live without it. Mind you, you work to sort of see a time when you don't have to do it but then you've built a life for everybody round it and you can relax a bit and still do bits of things that you enjoy. Not like some people seem to be so into work that they have to do it for some reason, and if they didn't do it they'd crack up.

Compared with many men, because he was a teacher and had the same holidays as his children, Chris did have some idea of what it was like to be totally responsible for child-care. This had led him to revise some of his opinions and also change certain things that he had been used to doing.

Kids are always demanding things and you've got so many things pulling you and you don't really know sometimes. And, at the end of the day, if you do spend all your time with them you feel a bit lost in some ways because you haven't done anything you wanted to do, so you feel a bit empty. You know, like holidays when you spend a week at home, my wife might work and I spend nearly all day with them. You're starting to seem inhuman after four or five days. I always thought that teaching wouldn't make me dependent on it but it does make you project yourself a bit more than you would normally if you were inside and at home. Where we live it's a bit like people get into their cars and shoot off and they don't lean over the fence and talk to each other so you don't see people unless you go out and make them talk to you. I can appreciate what it feels like for other people stuck at home all day. You know, when I used to come home I used to think, right, I've done my bit. I've done my work. I've made the money. Now I can do what I want to do. And the effect of that is you say, I want to go for a run or something. So I'd go home, thought I'd done my bit and go off for a run! And [your wife, or whoever is looking after the children] is still there, at home, in the same position and nobody else is with them. And I finally stop in the evening when I've been at home with them all day and I'm too tired to do anything at all and I'm not really inclined to. It's a funny situation and you often think if I'd done this differently would they have turned out differently? I don't know.

As Chris indicated, when it looked as if there was a danger that he might lose his family, he was rather surprised to find out how much they did actually mean to him. He returned to this theme and considered how his views on fatherhood had changed over the years. He also recognized some of the ways in which he had changed because he was a father.

To start with I think it was about providing for them and making sure that everything was all right for them. But that's not enough now. It's also about getting a lot back as well now. Realizing that what you are like is affected so much by them, it's not all that way. Just realizing that you can't imagine what it would be like if they weren't there any more, there's a lot of that. And when you reach that stage when you realize that you do care, I always used to think, well, I could take them or leave them, I've done my bit. I've filled my responsibility of doing this, this and this. Of providing the house and the food and everything and apart from that I could get away, I can live in another world. But things slowly get hold of you and they become a part of you and you realize that they are a lot more a part of you than you ever thought they were, and you can't go on without them, not when you get to this stage, you can't go on without them. I don't know what it is really. It's like a lot of things. I'm being willing to give something away because I know once I've given it away I can't get it back. And once you show you care for them you can't not care any more. And it felt like loads of that to start with. I thought I can't show I care too much. I don't know if it's something I got from the way I was brought up in some way, you know, not getting too involved because once you're involved you get hurt and if you just stand back then you won't get hurt at all. It's not a trust in people because I don't seem to have a lot of trust in people. Because I can't understand when people are really cold and do things deliberately to hurt people. I can't understand that because my parents were never like that. They couldn't be apparently on the surface saying one thing and really meaning something else. And that's something kids don't like. Kids are something else. You can't blame them for anything. They're sort of blameless. They're just there. I can really feel for them now. Because you've no right to affect them at all in any bad way, because they haven't done anything to deserve anything. But I felt really sort of possessive towards my children so I thought, well, they're a bit me now and they can't be forgotten about and they are individuals now, so it's a very funny feeling. It's not a stage I imagined getting to. I'd thought well, so many people seem to be living lives now where they split up and they see the kids sometimes and they live a separate life from their family's sometimes, and that seems to be the norm now. Now I can't imagine that. It would tear me apart. We'd reached that stage and I thought, we can't have this so we're trying to sort things out. But it's to do with time and the time you spend with people and the time you spend with your kids and the career thing. I really thought, well, this is a load of rubbish this. This is not what I want. And everything's connected and the problems that have been going on in this school have me even more convinced, God, what is this work, nothing. . . . I was off the first term this year, with pneumonia, and if you don't do anything else you think then and I felt well, people soon forget you. Your colleagues and things. You try to imagine you're irreplaceable and in some ways people always remember you and the kids will be saying, 'Where is he today? But once you're gone, other people do it. Other people do that job so you're not irreplaceable like that. But you are irreplaceable to the people at home. No one could ever be what you've been to them. You can't replace that.

But it wasn't just with regard to his own children that Chris had changed. In his view fatherhood had made him become much more sympathetic and understanding to his pupils and, by implication, to their parents.

I've been a lot more understanding. I always felt that I was, a bit, but I don't feel so superior if you like. I don't suppose I ever did really but with the kids at this school I don't feel that I've done it better and my kids aren't going to be like you any more like I did a bit at — school. I'll listen to anything now. About my own kids I thought, if after all the time you spend with them you can't get it right! You know? You think that, as an art teacher your children should be good at art, but they're not. There's a sense of failure there as well because if they don't live up to your expectations, which, as I've seen from our in-laws and things, you've got to show them that they're valued. The effect here, at school, is that I've been able to talk to them and not feel as if I was teaching them a lot more. I've seen them as human and not thinking, well, this lesson I've got to teach this, this and this and get that across and if they open their mouths to talk about anything else you shut them up quickly. I mean, just at the start of the day, when the kids come in, before you actually teach them, I used to begrudge that a bit but I've since been glad of it because they've come in, they've talked about, not about their lessons, they just talk about themselves and you find out a surprising lot. You know, a lad says his father's moved out and his mother's had to look after them and all this business and you can be very sympathetic to what they do in the rest of the day then. And by and large most kids have a lot more to put up with than the kids at home, my kids, because whatever we do we try to ensure that they don't suffer from whatever goes on.

Looking back at what he said twelve years ago it is possible to see the change that Chris describes. Then he was preoccupied with communicating ideas connected with the art he was teaching and one can imagine that he would have given short shrift to any interruptions.

It's difficult to start with, a challenge if you like, but I can see things . . . you know, goals, that I'd quite like to reach, being able to communicate successfully and so on . . . getting across certain complicated things you know, sort of ideas, being able to share those ideas, that are of a very complicated, sometimes personal nature. You just have to some way improve and cut down the time it takes you to get to some more important things that I am interested in and want to understand. . . . Everything's got to be so obvious and laid in front of them without any doubts about it . . . well most of the time, you can't leave too much that can be interpreted wrongly. . . . You have to plan and go through all the possibilities before, or at least work out what could happen . . . in terms of interpretation, the way they might interpret ideas that you're telling them . . . how they might misinterpret or the directions they might go off in from the ideas that you give them.[18]

Such a change is perhaps, partly to do with increasing maturity for there is evidence to suggest that as they get older teachers do become more concerned with pastoral work than with their subject. Nevertheless, as a father, Chris was in a better position to empathize with children's need to talk about themselves at least as much as about their school work. And he had also been able to draw on his home experiences to improve his pedagogy:

> The thing I've learnt a little bit more is to be able to play with kids,
> not just tell them what to do all the time but to play with them
> instead just – as I did tend to do with the teaching – direct them and
> stand back. You can't do that with kids at home. You have to be part of
> what they're doing. They don't want you to just say 'Go off and paint',
> they want you to be with them, doing it. Unfortunately I didn't realize
> that. I thought you could set them off and like sort of machines they'd
> keep going. But they don't want that. They want you there holding the
> brush and the paint and you can just forget about you and what you
> were planning to do that day. That doesn't matter. And I've taken
> something from that into school.

And so had his other colleagues who had their own children. In common with everyone else whom I spoke with Chris felt that one of the major differences between teachers who had children and those who didn't lay in their necessarily acquired capacity to relax and in their ability to be 'natural' with their pupils:

> I think those who don't have kids seem a lot tenser. You have to learn
> how to relax with your own kids. You can't be uptight with them all
> the time. You feel that the ones who've got their own are being real
> with the kids. You know they speak to their kids like that and they
> adopt that way of talking to the kids here. The others seem a bit, this
> is their job, you know, this is the only time they come into contact with
> kids, this is how they speak to them, and kids don't like that. They
> want to be treated as human beings, as individuals, and not told what
> to do all the time. Things have to be negotiated. You're calmer I think,

because you've had to be. It isn't something you can switch on and off. When you get home you have to be calmer and at the end you don't necessarily have to change when you get here.

Whilst he had an enhanced and more empathetic understanding of the needs and concerns of his pupils and of their parents, Chris could also see situations from the teacher's point of view. Being in such a position had forced him to adopt a wider and more complex perspective on children's behaviour than he had previously, for he could see that experiences both at school and at home were influential. This realization had been strengthened as a result of his own son's problems. His wife's response was, however, quite different, and Chris attributed this to the fact that she was not a teacher:

> We've visited primary school to talk about our kid and you get the impression, my wife still does, that the school blame us for whatever. We're held personally responsible for the behaviour of our son in school and their line is 'You can't help us here.' And you think, well, as a teacher you tend to blame the parents but when you're a parent *and* a teacher, who do you blame? There's nobody left so you think, yes, it's got to be a joint thing. But my wife doesn't feel it quite the same way. My wife blames the school all the time and reacts quite strongly. I can see the difficulties the school is working under. You have to treat the kids in a whole sort of way but because the class sizes are bigger you can't listen to the child when he wants to talk to you as you might be able to do with smaller classes because there's no time. I mean we've looked at what our son can do when problems occur. We've said 'Well, isn't there someone you can go and talk to? Isn't there a pastoral care system where you can just go and talk to them?' Well there isn't. The only pastoral care is the head and he's part of the problem. But here (in secondary school) we've got a pastoral care system and the people here could listen to children. But yes, we have an on-the-edge relationship with the school now because of the way we've perceived them dealing with an individual's needs. We can handle it at home so we suggest they adopt the way we handle it, which they can't do at school and it ends up being very frustrating. Because if we're saying you should reward positive behaviour, not mention all the negative things, and they say, 'Oh yes. We agree. We agree' but they don't do it because they haven't time to, they say they can only deal with problems when they arise, they can't deal with reinforcing positive behaviour all the time.

Of course, understanding the difficulties under which teachers labour does not necessarily ease the frustration and unhappiness felt by Chris, his wife and their son. It might, though, have helped them to secure some level of support because it did inform Chris's approach to the boy's head teacher:

My wife thinks they've listened to me more because I'm a teacher. My wife thinks that she's treated by the head in a very patronizing way because she's a woman and not a teacher. She's complained to the governors about it. I mean, she gets rung up at work and told that my son's kicked a girl in the face and broken her nose. So she rings me up to go up to school. By the time I get there it tends to be later in the day, when the headmaster's really calm and he says, 'Well, it was an accident really.' He's very reasonable and I go home and say 'Oh, there isn't a problem.' In school they seem to be under so much pressure that they seem to react in an instinctive way to things then when they can finally get hold of me and things have calmed and they've thought things through, they can be reasonable. You can't be reasonable when you're in the middle of it. And that seems to be the problem and I can appreciate that but when it's your child you can't be too sympathetic. I feel I know the struggle they have so I am prepared to compromise in what I think, because it's got to be about compromising all the time. So I don't go in saying, 'This is what I want. Why don't you do it?' as some parents do. I seem to go in and say, 'This is what I'd like to see. How can you do it? Can we have something like that?' And they say, 'Yes' and they respond and I know that they respond far better to somebody like that than to an aggressive approach. If you go in aggressively you get aggression back again.

I have tried throughout to avoid comparing Chris's perceptions and experiences as a father with those of the mother teachers I talked with. I kept telling myself that it would be a spurious comparison because he, and they, should primarily be regarded as individuals, each living different lives in different circumstances and coming from different backgrounds. I stated right at the beginning that it was not my intention to make generalizations. Any comparison on the grounds of sex cannot be anything other than a generalization. And yet, despite these prohibitions I cannot help making some observations that are based on what seem to me to be fundamental differences between Chris and the other men I talked with, and the women.

The women seemed to have more of a flow between the school and home part of their lives. It seemed to me that they, fluidly and in a taken-for-granted manner took things from home and being a mother, to school and being a teacher. This may have something to do with the mother-made-conscious ideology which dominates primary teaching so that there are many similarities between the ways in which the two roles and spheres are perceived and realized. However, it was also the same for the female secondary trained teachers. These women also saw close links between their two jobs, even though nothing in their initial teacher education had encouraged them to think in this way. Chris, however, appeared to have had to work so much harder to make the links. At one point he says that you respond to pupils in school in a certain way because you know it is likely to work but you don't think to adopt the same approach with regard to your children in school. Some feminists have suggested that women do take a more wholistic view of the world in general, not separating the different areas up into discrete compartments. This looks to be happening here.

It was noticeable that one theme to which Chris continually returned was that of how, when you have children, you can't so easily do what you personally want to do. This is as true for women as it is for men but women who are mothers tend not to mention it, or only do so in passing. Before they have children however, they seem to be as inclined to talk and think in terms of their right to pursue their own interests.[19] This was definitely true for me. It would seem though, that motherhood is synonymous with selflessness. Perhaps mothers think it would be oxymoronic to talk, as mothers, about their own time.

So far it sounds as if I am being critical of Chris as Chris. This is not my intention. He is talking as a father, with all the expectations and social meaning that that role involves. He is as much a prisoner of social circumstances as mothers are. And he recognizes it. He recognizes that his 'manly' behaviour towards his son may have caused the boy problems, he recognizes that his manly behaviour as a provider and breadwinner may have damaged his marriage. He is trying to do something about it.

So much for the differences. There are, as well, many similarities which, it could be argued, are to do with him being a parent. Like the women, he thinks about how fortunate his own children are compared with many that he teaches. He also feels more for his pupils than he did before his own children were born. He has become more relaxed and calmer and less likely to get worked up about 'insignificant' things. From what he says it would be my view that he had become a 'better' teacher over the years, partly because of increased maturity and greater experience but also because he had his own children.

Interviewing Chris was one of the most exciting experiences of my career as a researcher. It was interesting to meet someone years on, and to see how the experiences they had had in the interim had impacted on their lives and influenced their thinking. In my view, this revisiting of a life emphasised the value of life history method in charting the development of an individual's life and of their sense of self. Chris's identity had changed and had become that of a father. This had been as much a conscious choice as it was the result of biology. And the type of father that he was also owed a considerable amount to the historical climate in which he was living. Once again, life history allowed this to be seen.

JAMES'S STORY

At the time of our conversations James was working as a part-time science teacher in a secondary school. He was 38 and had a 5-year-old daughter, Ruby, and a 13-year-old stepson, Sean.

James had gone into teaching through what he now thought were,

misguided reasons. I had parents who were lecturers and . . . I
thought that I might end up doing some lecturing. I liked the idea of
working in higher education, of doing some teaching, having some
interaction with people and doing some work on my own. But then,
when I came to having a PhD place offered to me I just couldn't face
doing three years on a bit of work that nobody understood what it was
all about and I chose to go into teaching. I suppose I'd always enjoyed
education and I didn't make the distinction then that once you start
teaching something in secondary school it's far remote from anything
that's necessarily stimulating (subject wise) and a long way from your
own research. Although I suppose that I now appreciate very different
things about it, I think historically, what I had in mind was more
some sort of research than teaching. . . . Actually, the first year of
teaching I didn't enjoy at all really, I'd acquired a university place to
do archaeology but some time in the next year, when I started to do
outdoor pursuits, I enjoyed it much more, because I enjoyed the kids.
But I didn't like teaching. . . . I think a lot of the stuff we were teaching, teaching an integrated science course, was inappropriate for the
kids we were teaching it to. Whereas doing outdoor education I was
able to do things that the kids wanted to do and that I was interested
in and that was enjoyable.

As he had originally suspected when thinking that he might like to lecture,
it was the interaction part of teaching that James found so enjoyable. He didn't,
however, find this in the classroom but rather in the extra-curricular work that,
like so many young teachers, he soon got heavily involved in.

In the first few years I used to spend a lot of my own time, weekends
and evenings and things, doing outdoor education courses where often
I'd be working with kids, teaching them outdoor pursuits whilst I was
training. . . . I felt generally very positive about them, even the kids
that were difficult or weren't very good at doing their work, because
generally, outside school in other circumstances I got on OK. 99 per
cent of the kids, they've got a reasonable side. . . . That's why it's about
trying to find something that's relevant to them so that you can har-
ness that side of them.

Whilst he enjoyed working with youngsters, he had no desires to be a
father.

I never wanted to have children of my own at that stage. I'm not sure
why. I think perhaps the woman I was with then, she wasn't very

keen, I think that might have been the case but I knew that I was never that keen.

The issue of having children was, however, largely decided for him when he started a relationship with the woman he later married:

> When I went to live with L she had a 3-year-old boy, Sean, so from then on I had quite a lot of contact with children. I became a parent really. That was ten, eleven years ago.

James had been closely involved in raising Sean but, to his surprise, found that it wasn't until his own, biological, child was born that he identified with and involved himself in the 'generalized community'[20] of parents.

> It seems a long time ago now but I remember after Ruby was born, and for a period afterwards being absolutely amazed how there was a whole world that I really had been no part of, had no comprehension of until having her and going through the birth of my own child. Because, curiously enough it didn't really happen through bringing up my stepson and I don't know why that was. Perhaps it's something to do with just being a parent, with being totally responsible for somebody that's, well, not yours, but who you've brought into the world. A very different feeling than Sean. . . . I was very much aware that after having Ruby I would end up having conversations with people and a lot of involvement with people that I just know would never have happened before. It's just a complete sphere of life that I knew nothing about at all and had no interest in. . . . You find yourself talking about children a lot more, and about problems with kids but in a different way than you do as a teacher.

There are various reasons as to why this was the case but it is probably significant that James took on the task of being Ruby's main carer. In many respects therefore, his experience of parenthood was possibly more like that of most women than it was of the majority of men. He was certainly more involved in child care on a day-to-day basis than even Chris who had responsibility for his children during school holidays.

Like Karen and her husband, James and his wife had based their decision to 'reverse roles' on pragmatic concerns. Of course, the fact that James and Peter (Karen's husband) were actively willing to stay at home and look after children for at least part of the time is significant in that it indicates that their senses of self were strong enough to withstand any social criticism. Men are expected to be the breadwinners and to earn more money than their wives. Although changing employment (and unemployment) patterns and trends are challenging the 'normality' of this expectation, those who do not conform may feel uncomfortable because their masculinity may be called into question.[21] This was not, however, a problem for James.

> We decided that I should go part-time so I'd look after her half the time and we'd have a minder for the other half. Then when she got older she went to a nursery half time. It made sense in that L was earning more than I was and had had a break in her career anyway and didn't particularly want another one. So it was sensible from that point of view and also I was partly quite keen to have some time where I could actually dabble and do a few other bits and pieces and having been in education a long time I quite fancied doing a few things in a different sphere. . . . Quite a lot of the time I was involved in setting up a business, and myself and this other man and Ruby used to go around doing that and between us we used to be known as 'two men and a baby'.

Nevertheless, other people did find James's status as child-carer difficult to cope with:

> When Ruby was little I did, I do still do, some adult teaching in a women and toddlers, or parent and toddlers group which was all women, and me, and I took Ruby along. And in a way it was effectively set up like a glorified coffee morning except that my status in it was slightly different, although I was a man, because I was teaching some information technology. Some of the time it was just interacting, chatting with them and then, well, it probably might have been OK but a lot of the women there viewed men as not people to be looking after babies, it was a sort of aspiring working-class area, and thought that it was odd that I maybe cooked or changed nappies and things

James linked these women's views with social class. We discussed how it was somewhat ironic that in a working-class area where, nowadays, women's chances of getting work were better than men's, traditional notions of masculinity were so entrenched, to the detriment of both men and women. Commenting on studies of unemployment, Morgan suggests that,

> unemployment may have the consequence of accentuating gender differences and division of labour, although this may be as much to do with wider ideological expectations about the appropriate activities of women and men and less to do with straightforward notions of masculinity being challenged by the fact of unemployment.[22]

Following on from this point about ideological expectations, despite his involvement in child care, James recognized that he did not have to take it quite so seriously as most mothers do. This was partly because he was not doing it full time, but it could also have had something to do with the way in which he saw the baby 'slotting in' with his other activities. This view contrasts with that propounded by influential writers such as Penelope Leach who exhort mothers to make their children the centre of their lives and to slot other things in only if they have the time. The same requirement is not placed on fathers:

> Because I was involved in something else I had a lot to do anyway so looking after the baby just slotted in. I was glad it was that way because I did get a lot of enjoyment out of having her. Some of the time it was a nuisance but a lot of the time it was fun. . . . And I was still teaching in school half of the time. From that experience I would feel quite daunted if I thought I was at home, with her, by myself all week. I don't think I would manage it at all. I think I would find it very difficult.

As do most parents, mothers as well as fathers.

Before Ruby was born, James had already been a step-parent for around ten years. He therefore had a realistic idea of some of the implications involved in having a child. He and his wife thought hard about whether or not they should have another baby, being aware of what it would mean for how they spent their time as well as for their relationship with each other and with Sean.

> We had Ruby when Sean was about 9. We were undecided about whether to have our own children or not because we could see both sides because we had weekends where Sean went to his dad's, every other weekend, and we'd had a child for six years or so anyway. It's not like embarking upon a family when you've never had children and you don't know what's going to hit you, whereas we knew exactly the situation, the good points and the bad points and also the effect of L leaving work, on the pension and that sort of thing. And L decided that if she was going to have a child she had to have it by the time she was 35. We didn't make our mind up but then she got pregnant anyway. But she wouldn't have done if we hadn't been thinking about it because we'd stopped being careful and we were pleased when it happened. So it wasn't perhaps planned in a normal decision way.

An increasing number of people these days are involved in step-families and have experience of the special difficulties that can be associated with being a step-parent or step-child. Although he had come to love Sean, James felt that there was a fundamental difference in the ties between him and the boy and those between him and Ruby:

I felt strong responsibility for Sean but in a very different way from when it's your own. I used to think it strange when L said, if circumstances were such, she would be prepared to die to let Sean survive and I'd always thought, 'That's crap. You can always have more children so why kill yourself?' Whereas I can identify with that now.

This strength and depth of emotion is more usually associated with maternal love. Men clearly feel it too, or at least James was prepared to acknowledge it. Once again, this is probably related to his sense of self and the way in which he is comfortable to be seen as an actively caring and emotive parent.

Yet, in his early relationship with Sean, James initially adopted a teacherly approach. This was partly because he was conscious that he wasn't the boy's biological parent and also, perhaps, because of his inexperience. In effect Sean was James's first child and, like Chris with his first son, he had treated him in the only way that he knew how. Having said that, the situation that James came into was not an easy one and knowing how best to respond in such circumstances is difficult:

With Sean I'd inherited a situation where his behaviour in certain situations wasn't very good, because of overcompensation, and I did find that I adopted the approach of treating him like I treated the kids at school. And it was continually on my mind at that time, knowing that I was a step-parent and discussing with L whether I would behave the same if it was my own child, whether I'd see it in such black and white. Although funnily enough it's much easier with Ruby because I don't have to feel guilty. If I want to tell her off or be strict, I can do it and nobody's saying, 'Well, you wouldn't do that if it's not yours.' It's much harder if it's not your child and you're trying to gauge whether you're being fair or not.

Of course, in school the formal role of the teacher does allow a degree of 'strictness' towards other people's children. In the home though, things are different. It seems that, in what James says, an element of what might be described as 'ownership' is coming into play. As so many of the people I talked with noted, as a teacher you do have to be especially careful about how you treat other people's children because they don't 'belong' to you and because you are answerable for their well-being while they are in your care. James felt a similar, although more complex, responsibility for his step-son. This responsibility for Sean and, later, for Ruby, together with James's experience of being both a step- and a birth-parent had influenced him as a teacher. Most profoundly, and possibly partly as a consequence of Sean's difficult experiences, James found that he saw his pupils in a different light. Consequently he treated them somewhat differently:

[Having Sean and later Ruby] certainly made me realize, at some point, how much we as teachers, or how I, maybe was guilty of, on many occasions, not treating the kids as individuals. When you see it from the other side of the fence you see very much an individual with their own problems, quite complex lifestyles and capable of all sorts of upsets or different emotions connected with what they are doing in the classroom. Whereas from the other side, before, I think I was guilty in many cases, although I knew they were all individuals I didn't accept, maybe I was unaware of, how they can be grouped, how one groups them at the expense of their individual worries and concerns. How, I suppose, one can convey an unsympathetic way to an individual's problems. . . . It makes me more aware of individual circumstances I think. I can perhaps feel more, I can see more first-hand the damage that's been done to different kids and their development, and witness or hear about some of the awful situations that some kids are in or some of the dreadful things that they witness or set-ups they're in. And when you can see how much smaller events, how much lesser events have quite a big effect on your own kids, it's just horrible to think what sort of psychological damage that some of the kids have going on.

Thus, in contrast to when he used to profess the rhetoric that each child is an individual, he had really come to see and experience children as individuals and was, therefore, better able to empathize with their problems. Like every other parent teacher he could also identify much more closely with his pupils' parents. Since Sean had moved into the age group that he actually taught, his relationships with parents had got onto a mutual and more productive footing:

I've noticed at parents' evenings, since Sean's been a teenager, since he's been about 9, I can identify a lot more with the concerns of the parents, what they describe as the behaviour of the kids at home and trying to get them to work and trying to get them to do this and trying to get them to socialize or trying to get them to stay in or a whole range of different problems. And it's so much easier to identify with it but also to say 'Oh yes, we have that. I can say this to you and I know it's not easy, definitely. I can't do it myself.' It shows more understanding of their situation.

Inevitably being a step-parent also proved to be a bonus both in helping him to get on with parents in a similar situation and also in giving insight into the difficulties experienced by some step-children.

As a teacher of biology and also of Personal and Social Education, James had been able to use his experiences of having a child to inform and enhance the content of his teaching (although I'm not convinced by his claims to know what pregnancy and childbirth feel like!):

> I know that when Ruby was born and for a couple of years after that I had to teach sex education anyway and child development, birth of babies, and that certainly changed a lot of the way I did it. Because of my experiences and awareness that was dramatically different after being involved, which I wasn't with Sean. I taught a lot of these things before and I was really quite oblivious of a lot of the actual things that went on and what it felt like. I'm much more aware of teaching things like care during pregnancy or general birth, much more aware of the female point of view.

Much more useful though, on a day-to-day basis, was being able to observe closely the ways in which children learn and how they cope with the demands that teachers make upon them. The knowledge and understanding that James had gained from watching and helping Sean had, to some extent, informed his pedagogical practice.

> It's only more recently that having children has had an effect on my teaching, as Sean's got to be the same age as the kids I teach. I helped him revise for a science test and things and it has made me change some of the things that I do and the way that I do them. In actual fact though he seems much brighter than a lot of the kids that I teach here. The stuff Sean's doing and the way they do it isn't appropriate to what I have to teach at all, which may be the case for a lot of teachers in these sorts of schools. Their own kids are quite different.

Here James is alluding to the difference that he perceived between teachers' children and other kids. It was not that he saw teachers' kids as inherently more able but rather that he felt that their parents' professional training and experience tended to result in a particular type of upbringing. Thus, while they might be helped to be academically successful, they often were difficult to teach and were badly behaved at school. James put this down to over-stimulation at home. Karen and Chris had said something similar but they had also speculated that having teachers as parents could have a demystifying effect.

> I know other teachers do it and I'm guilty of it myself. You're continually aware of the need to stimulate the child in different ways, to interest them in different things, trying to get them to develop fairly quickly in different ways and if they are bored or misbehaving, rather than just tell them off, to distract them into doing something else more interesting. It's something that I think a lot of teachers' kids turn out to be very badly behaved in school because, at home, if

they're getting a bit bored with something, someone says, 'Oh, have you had a try at doing this?' or gives them that personal attention, diverts them onto something else, finds them something else stimulating to do rather than them not misbehaving but just put them in a situation where they're not being occupied or entertained. They expect you to entertain them. And I think that teachers' kids are definitely worse for that.

Another thing that James was aware of doing and which Chris also mentioned, was adopting a teacherly approach to discipline at home. Both men had come to see this as being inappropriate but it had taken them some time to 'override' their inclination to do it:

I think that, perhaps with Sean, no, probably with both: in the classroom situation there's always a feeling that if certain things go too far, if certain situations develop with certain kids it's important to really retrieve the situation, to get those kids back to behave in the way they did before if once they step over the line, over the mark. Now, that is different with your own kids and yet I think that on occasions I've been guilty of adopting that approach. Thinking that, oh, they must not get away with it because then it's gone for ever, it's slipped away, and then you won't be able to, just by reasoning with them, and it's more of a personal interaction with them, actually bring the situation back to where you want it. Which is what happens as a parent because there are all sorts of times when things that you normally want to happen can't possibly. It's different then. You have to reason and hopefully you'll manage it and sometimes you do manage it. But it's a mistake to treat discipline at home and at school in the same way, because it is different.

None of the mother teachers had talked in quite the same way about importing whole-class discipline strategies into the home. Although this does not mean that they had never done it, it is possible that, right from the start, their ideas about how they should discipline their own children were distinct from their professional thinking and practice. It might also be that 'official' notions of how mothers, and primary-school teachers for that matter, should approach discipline emphasise strategies by which the child should think that they themselves have decided to behave in the desired manner. Herein may lie a fundamental difference between the traditional stereotypes of men, fathers and male teachers as authoritarian and those which cast mothers, and women generally, as gentle and persuasive. Neither James nor Chris were comfortable with the traditional role and had, therefore, come to question it as a result of their experiences of having their own children. In fact, partly as a result of simply getting older and reflecting on his life so far, but primarily because of having Ruby and Sean, James felt that, in some respects, he had become quite a different person:

> It has changed me. Or certainly I have changed, though I probably
> would have changed to some extent anyway, with age and experience.
> And one way that I have changed quite a bit is through studying quite
> a lot about psychotherapy and through some of the factors that have
> affected us since childhood and some of the differences between males
> and females and how they affect you from childhood. Consequently
> my interactions with women and with men have been on a very differ-
> ent level because of that. Now how much some of that has perhaps
> been through the position of having a child with me or having that
> experience I don't know, but it certainly affects the way that I am with
> my own children now. The awareness of how much damage happened
> to us in childhood. You see, both L and myself come from families
> where there have been major traumas and I've started to unravel
> some of the psychological damage that's happened to ourselves. L's
> dad committed suicide when she was 14, 15. Teenage years when she
> completely blamed herself for that. And I come from a family where
> my father was alcoholic so that for quite a few of my teenage years
> either both my parents were in hospital and I lived with somebody
> else or I was bringing myself up. It's highly likely that I would be
> involved in unravelling some of these things anyway, but having had
> the children has made me much more aware of the effect that it has
> on how they develop.

Clearly James's early life had not been easy or 'normal'. Now, as an adult, he was able to draw on his experiences to inform what he did both as a parent and as a teacher. In addition, having the opportunity to observe closely how his own children coped with difficulties and upsets gave him extra insight and helped him, in his opinion, to be a 'better' teacher.

Everybody's story is interesting and in some respects unique. What made James's story special was its unconventional aspects and the way in which it was more like a woman's than a man's. I have to be honest and say that I heard and interpreted it comparatively whereas with Chris and the other men I talked to, it was the differences which initially seemed to stand out.

Plenty of women take advantage of the opportunities teaching offers to com-bine child care with work but not many men do. There are often financial reasons for this but the social pressures to conform do play an important part. James, however, had no regrets and, in opting for the part-time route, felt that he had gained by having the chance to develop an especially strong relationship with his daughter. Indeed he had the sort of relationship that is usually reserved for mothers and he spoke about this in strong emotional terms. Talking in this way is, in itself, something that it more usual for women than it is for men.

In school James made no secret of the way in which he organized his life. His pupils knew why he was part-time, so consequently his identity as a teacher incorporated the fact that he was a father. He also explicitly used his family experiences as content and illustration for his biology and Personal and Social Education lessons. He was not, therefore, guilty of 'repudiat(ing) the intimacy of nurture in (his) own histor(y) and (his) work in education'.[23] He might even have provided a role model for his pupils, and for his colleagues too.

Perhaps it was easier for James to do this than it would be for other male teachers because he had little to lose in terms of career development; in this respect as well, his position mirrored that of many women. In choosing to work part time he had chosen to remain at a relatively junior level. Indeed, if he decided to return to full-time work at a later stage it is possible that he would face even more difficulty than women returners do, simply because he had taken such an unusual line for a man. For fathers as much as mothers the rewards of active parenthood often have to be intrinsic rather than extrinsic ones!

NOTES

1   Plummer, K., *Telling Sexual Stories: Power, Change and Social Worlds,* London, Routledge, 1995.
2   Casey, K., *I Answer With My Life: Life Histories of Women Teachers Working For Social Change,* New York, Routledge, 1993, pp. 107–53.
3   Ibid, p. 109.
4   Ibid.
5   Mac an Ghaill, M., *Young, Gifted and Black,* Milton Keynes, Open University, 1988.
6   Casey, op. cit.93.
7   Ibid, p. 124.
8   Ibid.
9   David, M., Edwards, E., Hughes, M. and Ribbens, J., *Mothers and Education: Inside Out? Exploring Family, Educational Policy and Experience,* Basingstoke, MacMillan, 1993, p. 115.
10 Measor, L. and Sikes, P., *Gender and Schools,* London, Cassells, 1992, pp. 111–13.
11 Sikes, P., Measor, L. and Woods, P., *Teacher Careers: Crises and Continuities,* Lewes, Falmer, 1985.
12 Sikes, P., 'The Life Cycle of the Teacher' in Ball, S. and Goodson, I. (eds), *Teachers' Lives and Careers,* Lewes, Falmer, 1985, p. 45.
13 Sikes, Measor and Woods, *op. cit.*, p. 26.
14 Erickson, E., 'Identity and the Life Cycle', *Psychological Issues* 1, 1959.
15 Jung, C., *The Portable Jung* (ed. Joseph Campbell), New York, Viking Press, 1971.
16 Levinson, D. with Darrow, C., Klein, G., Levinson, M. and McKee, B., *The Seasons of a Man's Life,* New York, Alfred A. Knopf, 1979.
17 Sikes, *op. cit.*, p. 52.
18 Ibid, pp. 35–6.
19 Ibid.
20 Plummer, *op. cit.*, p. 37.
21 See Morgan, D., *Discovering Men,* London, Routledge, 1992, pp. 99–119.

22 Ibid, p. 117.
23 Grumet, M., *Bitter Milk: Women and Teaching,* Amherst, University of Massachusetts Press, 1988, p. xvi.

Chapter 6

Conclusion
'There's Thousands of Us Out There'

INTRODUCTION

My intention in writing this book has not been to construct icons of parent teacherhood in which many teachers who are parents fail to recognize their own experiences. Nor do I wish to claim that parents make the 'best' teachers. Rather what I want to do is to acknowledge that some of the knowledge, skills and understandings which can accrue from the experience of motherhood specifically, and parenthood more generally, cannot but help to have a positive impact upon how many, if not most teachers who are parents, teach. At least, this is the impression I gained from listening to the stories and working on the life histories of the mother and father teachers I spoke with.

At any one time, the majority of teachers are likely to be parents, although this has to be a supposition because figures to support such a claim cannot be obtained. Any 'special' contribution parent teachers do make to the job should, therefore, be recognized, considered and exploited by managers at all levels: from head teachers through to local and national policy-makers.

COMMON STORIES

I embarked upon this research because I wanted to know if other people had experienced the same emotional upheavals, the same shifts in their thinking and changes in their world-view, with similar consequences for their professional practice, as I had when I became a parent. I wanted to hear other parent teachers' stories because I had the idea that hearing these and attempting to understand them would help me to better understand what had happened to me. To paraphrase Plummer, I thought that I might be able to find something of myself and of my experience in the text of these stories.[1] I therefore had to collect the stories and it was this need, together with the personal and intimate genesis and nature of my research questions, that influenced my choice of a narrative, life history approach.

And what did I find? Well, basically I found that it had been the same for other people. Mother and father teachers alike were all unequivocally certain that their professional perceptions and practices had fundamentally changed, for the better, as a result of having their own children. I do have to emphasise, however, that these changes were all self-reported. I was only able to observe a few of the teachers at work and actually teaching. In any case though, I would have had to have seen them teaching pre- and post-children in order to begin to gain a sense of any concrete change. But I do not think that the lack of 'objective' evidence matters. What I wanted to know was whether the teachers subjectively and qualitatively felt any difference: that they said that they did is, therefore, sufficient.

Of course, parenting is differentially experienced and everyone I listened to told me their own, idiosyncratic story. Details varied because parents live in different circumstances, conditions and contexts; they are motivated by different values and imperatives; they have different backgrounds and experiences upon which to draw; and their children have different temperaments and needs. As Hirsch argues,[2] with reference to mothers, we need to acknowledge 'difference within the feminine and multiple difference within the maternal', and the same is true for fathers and for parents more generally. Similarly, teachers are by no means an homogeneous group with regard to any aspect or dimension of their experience or practice. And yet, despite these differences, all the informants spoke in similar terms about their basic shared experience, namely of being a teacher who is also a parent, and vice versa. Like Kathleen Casey I found that 'important common verbal patterns do emerge within the narratives of (a) particular social group of teachers in particular social circumstances'.[3] There does seem to be a 'generalized'[4] or 'interpretive'[5] community of parent teachers who draw on a 'general cultural repertoire'[6] to talk about such things as the way in which they see their own children reflected in their pupils, their increased patience, tolerance and empathy, the effect that their professional training has had upon them as parents, and the way in which their family becomes their over-riding commitment and priority. This is, no doubt, to a greater or lesser extent, a consequence of having been exposed to similar ideologies of parenting and of teaching and of living through the same historical times. By virtue of my own exposure and my own membership of this community and on the basis of what parent teachers who have read draft copies of this book told me, I am relatively confident that I clearly heard, recognized and interpreted what was being said as was intended. For instance Sian said,

> I couldn't put it down from start to finish because it was my story that I was reading. (*Sian*)

Sue commented,

> I couldn't stop reading it. I'd been busy all week and I hadn't had a chance to look at your MS. Then on Thursday I went upstairs to do some tidying up and it was on the desk. I started reading it and I couldn't stop. It's about our generation, there's thousands of us out there. (*Sue*)

Even so I take full responsibility for how I have re-presented and re-interpreted what I was told.

I also have to accept the way in which the simple invitation of being asked to talk about the possible influences that being a parent had upon people's perceptions and experiences as teachers, sent out certain messages. For a start people knew that I was favourably disposed to parent teachers. They could also work out that I held a unitary view of the person and believed that personal, professional and public experiences and aspects of life inevitably interacted with each other. Consequently people may have told me particular versions of their stories because they thought that this was what I wanted to hear. Indeed, some of the mother teachers actually told me that they would have given quite different accounts of how and where their children fitted into their lives, in settings where such information might have implications for their career development, or more specifically, for their promotion prospects. Similarly father teachers told me that they rarely mentioned their children at school because they were not expected to; they did not feel that that part of their life was seen, by their superiors or by society in general, to be of significant relevance to their teaching.

Despite the fact that a number of people told me that they felt it was artificial to compartmentalize their lives into public and professional, personal and private, the existence of these different versions of their stories does raise questions concerning the 'truth' of what I was told. But perhaps truth, as it is normally understood is not a relevant concept here. Like Ken Plummer I too 'have slowly come to believe that no stories are true for all time and space . . . (and) that multiple stories engulf us, and we need tools for distinguishing between layers of stories, or even layers of truth'.[7] Perhaps one such 'tool' might just be the explicit recognition that people often do have to work to separate their selves and aspects of their lives in order to cope with the different requirements of the various social contexts in which they are involved.

With regard to teachers, there is quite a large body of work which does look at coping strategies of this kind.[8] What my own research highlighted for me, however, was the deceptiveness and the hypocrisy of the public teacher/private parent split. This is because being a parent is undeniably a public and a political matter. The recent attention that has been given to the so-called breakdown of the family as the major cause of social disorder makes this absolutely plain. Teachers, likewise, have been excoriated for what is seen as their part in the creation of a disenchanted, ill-disciplined, anti-social and alienated generation. Parent teachers, therefore, can come in for double criticism, or even more if they are mother teachers who leave their children in order to go out to work! Yet analyses of such a simplistic and precise nature are of little value when it comes to wider social problems. Structures, institutions and ideologies supported by a complex web of social interactions, rather than individuals or specific groups of individuals are more likely to be at the root of things. Making a space for individuals to tell their stories or, as some people term it, 'giving voice' can help to clarify this by revealing that people live their lives and make sense of them in circumstances which are not of their own choosing. Describing these circumstances and contextualizing the stories can also make it clear that individuals, or the groups they belong to, do not on their own, bear the responsibility.[9]

There are obvious links between parenting and teaching, links which to a great extent have been suppressed and denied. Educationalists, academics and policy-makers have all made connections, of various kinds, between mothering and teaching little children and also between the traditional authoritarian, patriarchal style of fathering and the disciplining of children. These connections, however, are very much within the terms of the dominant ideologies of both parenting and teaching, and they serve to reinforce hierarchies in which mothering and nurturance tends only to be rhetorically valued. The well-rewarded posts and positions of authority and influence usually go to those who employ and display other characteristics. The teachers I talked with wanted, however, to shift the emphasis and to have their parenting experiences, and the way in which these experiences could enhance their professional practice, acknowledged. At the present time the parent teachers felt that they actively had to keep quiet about that aspect of their lives if they wanted to maintain a professional identity. The exceptions were those fortunate enough to come into contact with head teachers, like Sylvia and Karen, who had reached a personal and professional position in which they felt sufficiently confident to publicly acknowledge the special contribution that parents who are teachers can make. Ironically though, these women had, to some extent, had to play down the fact that they had children in order to get into that position! They felt strongly that it should not have to be like that. At this point it does, therefore, seem appropriate to consider some of the policy implications that follow from recognizing that being a parent can enrich and enhance professional practice.

POLICY IMPLICATIONS

Actually being a teacher and a parent is not always that easy. For many people, especially for women, the decision to have a child has tended to mean accepting that their career might not develop as far or as fast as it might otherwise have done. Of course, teaching is not unique in this respect and in Britain there is legislation aimed at preventing discrimination on the basis of parenthood. Nevertheless, as we have seen, attitudes towards working parents, and mothers in particular, are often not conducive to career continuance, let alone development. Even though it has often been said, it is worth repeating that there needs to be even more flexible thinking about, and generous provision of:

- maternity/paternity leave;
- job sharing;
- part-time and supply work;
- 'refresher' courses for returners;

- child-care provision of various kinds (e.g. full-time and before-school and after-school clubs);
- opportunities for parent teachers to take time off to look after sick children without being punitively treated.

Initiatives based on the above do exist at both local and national level but they do not reach everyone who might benefit from them. To a large extent, what is available in any area depends upon the efforts of committed individuals. For instance, in England and Wales, monies and other types of assistance have been available from central government to set up reasonably priced before-school and after-school child care based in schools. Many parent teachers would welcome and would make use of such provision but take-up has been patchy. One of my informants, Stuart, together with parent teacher colleagues, tried, unsuccessfully, to persuade his head teacher (himself the father of a teenager) of the benefits of setting up such a scheme. The head's view was that it was the teachers' private responsibility to have their children cared for and that it had nothing at all to do with their work. Such views are by no means unusual.

Although there is not any objective evidence to support the assertion, observation and personal reports suggest that, clearly, the vast majority of parent teachers do make adequate and expensive private arrangements to have their children looked after while they work. They do this because they are committed to their job.[10] Their pupils, therefore, benefit from their experience and expertise, but at a financial, and often emotional, cost to the teacher. More part-time opportunities and child care facilities, possibly based in schools, would enable many more teachers to work and to look after their children in the proportions that they are most happy with. If, as I am suggesting, parent teachers do bring something of value to their work this should be formally recognized, their contribution acknowledged and their needs accommodated. At school level, some head teachers are making policy and organizational decisions which do go some way towards doing this. Sylvia and Karen are not alone in drawing on their own experiences as mothers to try and make things easier both for their members of staff who have children as well as for their pupils' parents.

Whilst head teachers clearly do have considerable influence over what happens in their own institutions, for teaching generally, to become a parent-friendly occupation there needs to be action and development at a national level. Such action and development would require financial investment, but before this is likely to happen politicians have to be convinced of the 'added value' that parent teachers can bring. In England and Wales, in the early 1990s, there were signs that there was some official recognition of this for it was proposed to introduce a 'mum's army' of 'mature', quickly trained, relatively low-paid, early-years teachers. Admittedly this plan was largely an attempt to save money on teacher education but it did, nevertheless, at least acknowledge that parents, or more specifically, mothers, had something to offer. However, the proposal, as it was originally framed, was never realized. Teachers' organizations, educationalists and parents objected strongly to what appeared to be an attempt to lower both the status of early-years teachers themselves and the education they provide. Drafting mothers in to teach little children for less money than teachers of older kids seems, in some ways, to denigrate, rather than value, the contribution their parenting experience can make to their professional role. It also reinforces gender stereotypes. That, for whatever reason, the politicians heeded the objections of teachers, parent teachers and parents is positive. However, there is still a long way to go and more stories need to be told and heard before teachers can really feel that their parenting experiences are officially seen as having any professional worth.

A STORY FOR THE TIMES

In his writing about stories and power, Plummer suggests that 'stories live in (the) flow of power. The power to tell a story, or indeed not to tell a story, under the conditions of one's own choosing, is part of the political process.'[11] Plummer argues that when social worlds change then the nature and type of stories which are told and which it is possible to tell changes too. It may be that the time for stories of parenting and parent teacherhood specifically, has come. Others in other parts of the world (e.g. Madeline Grumet, Kathleen Casey, Robert Bullough) are telling such stories and the limited evidence suggests that they are being received positively. At any rate they are being published and hence, one imagines, being read and heard. Perhaps the time for a more positive perspective on parenting and on the contribution that the subjective and emotional can make in areas of life which have traditionally been defined as objective and professional has also arrived. After all, the interaction has always been there; it has just not been acknowledged. Part of the reason for this may be to do with the political nature and implications of parenthood in general and mothering in particular. Mothering, according to the dominant ideologies, limits women's opportunities to participate in public life and to take up positions of power. If you are being an 'ideal' mother there is no space for you to do anything else because you are totally concerned with the needs of your child. Similarly, traditional notions of nurturance demand absolute commitment to the needs of others. Taking on such roles and responsibilities, or being expected to conform to them, circumscribes the world.

In their fight for equality some groups of feminists have tended to deprecate mothering because they see it as contributing to women's subordination. Others have presented it as a series of irreconcilable dichotomies. I prefer to follow Casey who writes that there is a need for those who are concerned with education to move beyond such an antithetical conceptualization and who quotes,

> Martin (1985) (who) argues that 'theories of curriculum will be more complete' when 'the activities of family living and child-rearing' are recognized as worthwhile. Such a project would necessitate the radical reconstruction

of existing norms of the maternal, and of curriculum; as Ruddick (1984) has argued, we need 'to bring a transformed maternal thought into the public realm, to make the preservation and growth of all children a work of public conscience and legislation'.[12]

I would want to take this further to explicitly include pedagogical theories and practices as well as theories of curriculum. I also would want to press for a radical reconstruction of existing norms of the paternal for it seems to me that maternal norms cannot be reconstructed on their own. Maybe both projects are already under way, albeit quietly and slowly. On the basis of my own research I think that there is some room for optimism for I have to confess to being surprised by the similarities in what the father and mother teachers had to say about parenting and children and about how their feelings towards children had changed once they became parents. My surprise is, perhaps, an indication of the strength of the ideologies and the 'effectiveness' of my own socialization concerning stereotypical gender roles. Yet some fathers have always been happy to take on a nurturing role towards children. My own father and his father before him, were eager to look after their own and other people's babies, at least in the home. They were also quite happy to be seen out in the street, pushing prams in historical times (the early 1900s in the case of my grandfather), when this was far from a normal activity for men. Of course, that my father was happy to change nappies owes something to the environment in which he grew up and where he saw his own father doing such things. My father-in-law, on the other hand, felt that showing physical affection to his sons was likely to have detrimental effects on their masculinity. He was also concerned about any signs of his boys behaving 'inappropriately'. For instance, he expressed extreme disquiet and fear when my husband (aged 6) tucked his Sooty glove puppet up in bed. David woke the next morning to find that the little bear had gone for good. Sadly, such stories are not uncommon for it is through experiences like this that boys learn how they should behave, and that the overt expression of nurturance and concern for others is not for them.

It is my view that caring for and looking after people in general and, with especial reference to teachers, children in particular, is one of, if not the most, important and valuable social interactions that there can be. Schools and teachers, in their prospectuses and in their personal statements of intent, usually claim that their aim is to help each child to achieve their full potential. Whether or not this is just rhetoric, I believe that it remains the case that nurturance is necessary for the achievement of this aim. And yet various obstacles stand in the way which hinder the development of a nurturing environment. Chief amongst these, in my view, is the notion and convention that nurturing behaviour is not necessarily appropriate in school, but that non-emotional, objective and 'masculine' behaviour is. This notion gains expression through the hierarchies and systems of all kinds by which schools and teachers tend to be organized and managed. Displaying nurturing behaviour, and/or drawing on the experience that comes from being a parent and living intimately and closely with children, being aware of some of their concerns and of the concerns of their parents, are not usually given any formal recognition or value. The teachers I talked with did think that these things were important though, and that they should be taken into account by policy-makers.

WHAT IF?

Whilst I am sceptical of the extent to which research can be 'empowering' or emancipatory[13] I do feel that making stories public makes it 'easier' for, or more likely that, other people will also tell a similar story, thus giving a certain status to their experiences. It also, obviously, potentially brings the stories to the attention of a wider audience, although there can be no guarantee about how various members of this audience will interpret them. Publicizing stories also, and at the same time, provides a template or plot by which other people can interpret their lives. Just as I hoped to find and come to a better understanding of myself in my respondents' stories, so other people can look at these stories and maybe find themselves, or aspects of themselves, in them too. In so doing they might be prepared to publicly acknowledge the part that being a parent plays in their lives. If more people do speak out then parenting may come to occupy a more valued position than it presently seems to do. What might this mean? I will leave you with a question posed by Barbara Rothman:

> What if we genuinely valued that work that is motherhood? What if we valued intimacy and nurturance, and human relationships, not just as a means towards an end, but in themselves? Would such a valuing privilege women as mothers – but simultaneously lock out non-mothering women and all men? I genuinely do not think so. Such a valuing would open up, and not close down, acts of nurturance and caring, free up, and not constrain, the gender boundaries of intimacy we now face, It would expand, and not restrict, the very definition of mothering.[14]

NOTES

1   Plummer, K., *Telling Sexual Stories: Power, Change and Social Worlds,* London, Routledge, 1995, p. 21.
2   Hirsch, M., *The Mother/Daughter Plot: Narrative, Psychoanalysis, Feminism,* Bloomington, Indiana University Press, 1989.
3   Casey, K., *I Answer With My Life: Life Histories of Women Teachers Working For Social Change,* New York, Routledge, 1993, p. 26.
4   Cf. Plummer, *op. cit.*, p. 37.
5   Fish, S., *Is There a Text in This Class? The Authority of Interpretative Communities,* Cambridge, Harvard University Press, 1980.
6   Popular Memory Group, 'Popular Memory: Theory, Politics, Method', in Johnson, R., McLennan, G., Schwarz, B. and Sutton, D. (eds), *Making Histories,* London, Hutchinson, 1982.

7   Plummer, *op. cit.*, p. 170.
8   See, for example, Hargreaves, A., 'Dissonant Voices, Dissipated Lives: Teachers and the Multiple Realities of Restructuring', Paper presented at 6th International Conference of ISATT, University of Gothenburg, Sweden, 1993; Nias, J., *Primary Teachers Talking: A Study of Teaching as Work,* London, Routledge, 1989; Pollard, A., 'A Model of Classroom Coping Strategies', *British Journal of Sociology of Education* 3, 1, 1982; Sparkes, A., 'Physical Education Teachers and the Search for Self: Two Cases of Structured Denial', in Armstrong, N. (ed.), *New Directions in Physical Education,* Vol. 3, London, Cassells, 1995; Woods, P., *The Divided School,* London, Routledge & Kegan Paul, 1979.
9   Sikes, P., Measor, L. and Woods, P., *Teacher Careers: Crises and Continuities,* Lewes, Falmer, 1985.
10 See Measor, L. and Sikes, P., *Gender and Schools,* London, Cassells, 1992, pp. 111–13.
11 Plummer, *op. cit.*, p. 26.
12 Casey, K., 'Teacher as Mother: Curriculum Theorizing in the Life Histories of Contemporary Women Teachers', *Cambridge Journal of Education,* 20, 3, 1990, p. 302.
13 See Sikes, P., Troyna, B. and Goodson, I., 'Talking About Teachers: A Conversation About Life History', *Taboo: The Journal of Culture and Education,* Vol. 1, Spring 1996.
14 Rothman, B. K., 'Beyond Mothers and Fathers: Ideology in a Patriarchal Society', in Glenn, E. N., Chang, G. and Forcey, L. R., *Mothering: Ideology, Experience and Agency,* London, Routledge, 1994, p. 154.

References

Andrews, J., *In Praise of the Anecdotal Woman: Motherhood and a Hidden Curriculum*, Stoke-On-Trent, Trentham Books, 1994.

Badinter, E., *The Myth of Motherhood*, trans. R. DeGaris London, Souvenir Press, 1981 edition.

Balint, A., 'Love For the Mother and Mother Love', in Balint, A. (ed.), *Primary Love and Psychoanalytic Technique,* New York, Liveright Publishing Company, pp. 91–108.

Ball, S., 'Self-doubt and Soft-data: Social and Technical Trajectories in Ethnographic Fieldwork', *International Journal of Qualitative Studies in Education* 3, 2, 1990, pp.151-71.

Barone, T., 'Persuasive Writings, Vigilant Readings, and Reconstructed Characters: The Paradox of Trust in Educational Storysharing' in Hatch, J. A. and Wisniewski, R. (eds), *Life History and Narrative*, New York, Falmer, 1995, pp. 63–74.

Benn, C., 'Preface' in DeLyon, H.and Widdowson Migniuolo, F. (eds), *Women Teachers: Issues and Experiences,* Milton Keynes, Open University Press, 1989.

Bennett, A., *Writing Home*, London, Faber & Faber, 1994.

Bloom, L. and Munro, P., 'Conflicts of Selves: Non unitary Subjectivity in Women Administrators' Life History Narratives' in Hatch, J. and Wisniewski, R. (eds), *Life History and Narrative*, London, Falmer, 1995, pp. 99–112.

Board of Education, *Report of the Departmental Committee on the Training of Teachers for Public Elementary Schools,* London, HMSO, 1925.

Brown, G. and Desforges, C., *Piaget's Theory – A Psychological Critique,* London, Routledge & Kegan Paul, 1979.

Bruner, J., *Actual Minds, Possible Worlds,* Cambridge MA, Harvard University Press, 1986.

Burgess, H. and Carter, B., 'Bringing Out the Best In People: Teacher Training and the 'Real' Teacher,' *British Journal of Sociology of Education* 13, 3, 1992, pp. 349–59.

Burgess, R., 'Teacher Careers in a Comprehensive School' in Green, A. and Ball, S. (eds), *Progress and Equality in Comprehensive Education,* London, Routledge, 1988.

Casey, K., 'Teacher as Mother: Curriculum Theorizing in the Life Histories of Contemporary Women Teachers,' *Cambridge Journal of Education* 20, 3, 1990, pp.301-20.

Casey, K., *I Answer With My Life: Life Histories of Women Teachers Working For Social Change,* New York, Routledge, 1993.

Central Advisory Council for Education, *Children and Their Primary Schools (The Plowden Report)*, London, HMSO, 1967.

Chodorow, N., *The Reproduction of Mothering: Psychoanalysis and the Sociology of Gender,* Berkeley, University of California Press, 1978.

Clandinin, D., 'Developing Rhythm in Teaching: The Narrative Study of a Beginning Teacher's Personal, Practical Knowledge of Classrooms', *Curriculum Inquiry* 19, 1989, pp. 121–41.

Clarke, K., 'Public and Private Children: Infant Education in the 1820s and 1830s' in Steedman, C., Urwin, C. and Walkerdine, V. (eds), *Language, Gender and Childhood*, London, Routledge & Kegan Paul, 1985.

Clough, P., *The End(s) of Ethnography,* London, Sage, 1992.

Cohen, D., *Piaget – Critique and Reassessment,* London, Croom Helm, 1983.

References

Connell, R., *Teachers' Work*, Sydney, Allen & Unwin, 1985.

Cortazzi, M., *Primary Teaching How It Is: A Narrative Account*, London, David Fulton, 1991.

Cosslett, T., *Women Writing Childbirth: Modern Discourses of Motherhood*, Manchester, Manchester University Press, 1994.

Cotterill, P. and Letherby, G., 'Weaving Stories: Personal Auto/Biographies in Feminist Research', *Sociology* 27, 1, 1993, pp.67–80.

David, M., Edwards, E., Hughes, M. and Ribbens, J., *Mothers and Education: Inside Out? Exploring Family, Educational Policy and Experience*, Basingstoke, MacMillan, 1993.

de Beauvoir, S., *The Second Sex*, trans. and ed. H. Parshley London, Cape, 1953.

Denzin, N. and Lincoln, Y. (eds), *Handbook of Qualitative Research*, California, Sage, 1994.

Edginton, M., 'No Greater Kingdom', *Mother and Home*, November, 1948, pp. 44–5.

Elbaz, F., 'Knowledge and Discourse: The Evolution of Research on Teacher Thinking' in Day, C., Pope, M. and Denicolo, P. (eds), *Insight Into Teachers' Thinking*, Basingstoke, Falmer, 1990.

Emihovich, C., 'Distancing Passion: Narratives in Social Science' in Hatch, J. A. and Wisniewski, R. (eds), *Life History and Narrative*, New York, Falmer, 1995, pp. 37–48.

Erickson, E., 'Identity and the Life Cycle', *Psychological Issues* 1, 1959, pp. 1–171.

Evans, M., 'Reading Lives: How the Personal Might Be Social,' *Sociology* 27, 1, 1993, pp. 5–13.

Everingham, C., *Motherhood and Modernity*, Buckingham, Open University Press, 1994.

Fine, M., 'Working the Hyphens: Reinventing the Self and Other in Qualitative Research', in Denzin, N. and Lincoln, Y. (eds), *The Handbook of Qualitative Research*, London, Sage, 1994.

Firestone, S., *The Dialectic of Sex*, London, Cape, 1970.

Fish, S., *Is There a Text in This Class? The Authority of Interpretative Communities*, Cambridge, Harvard University Press, 1980.

Fonow, M. and Cook, J., *Beyond Methodology: Feminist Scholarship as Lived Research*, Bloomington, Indiana University Press, 1991.

Gieves, K. (ed.), *Balancing Acts: On Being a Mother*, London, Virago.

Gieves, K., 'Introduction' in Gieves, K. (ed.), *Balancing Acts: On Being a Mother*, London, Virago, 1989.

Gimenez, M., 'Feminism, Pronatalism and Motherhood' in Treblicott, J. (ed.), *Mothering: Essays in Feminist Theory*, Maryland, Rowman & Littlefield, 1983, pp. 287–314.

Gitlin, A. and Myers, B., 'Beth's Story: The Search for the Mother Teacher' in McLaughlin, D. and Tierney, W. (eds), *Naming Silenced Lives: Personal Narratives and Processes of Educational Change*, New York, Routledge, 1993.

Glenn, E., 'Social Constructions of Mothering: A Thematic Overview' in Glenn, E., Chang, G. and Forcey, L. (eds), *Mothering: Ideology, Experience and Agency*, New York, Routledge, 1994.

Glenn, E., Chang, G. and Forcey, L. (eds), *Mothering: Ideology, Experience and Agency*, New York, Routledge, 1994.

Glesne, C. and Peshkin, A., *Becoming Qualitative Researchers: An Introduction*, New York, Longman, 1992.

Good Housekeeping, *Good Housekeeping's Baby Book*, London, National Magazine Company Ltd, 1957.

Goodson, I., 'Life History and the Study of Schooling', *Interchange* 11, 4, 1981, pp. 62–76.

Goodson, I., 'Studying Teachers' Lives: An Emergent Field of Inquiry' in Goodson, I. (ed.), *Studying Teachers' Lives*, London, Routledge, 1992.

Goodson, I., 'The Story So Far: Personal Knowledge and the Political' in Hatch, J. A. and Wisniewski, R. (eds), *Life History and Narrative*, New York, Falmer, 1995, pp. 89–98.

Gramsci, A., *Selections From the Prison Notebooks*, (eds Q. Hoare and Nowell-Smith) London, Lawrence & Wishart, 1971.

Griffiths, M., '(Auto)Biography and Epistemology', *Educational Review* 47, 1, 1995, pp. 75–88.

Grumet, M., *Bitter Milk: Women and Teaching,* Amherst, University of Massachusetts Press, 1988.

Grumet, M., 'The Politics of Personal Knowledge' in Withering, C. and Nodding, N. (eds), *Stories Lives Tell: Narrative and Dialogue in Education,* Columbia New York, Teachers' College Press, 1991, pp. 67–77.

Halpin, D. and Troyna, B. (eds), *Researching Educational Policy: Ethical and Methodological Issues,* London, Falmer, 1994.

Hammersley, M. and Atkinson, P., *Ethnography: Principles in Practice,* London, Routledge, 1989.

Hargreaves, A., *Changing Teachers, Changing Times: Teachers' Work and Culture in the Postmodern Age,* London, Cassell, 1994.

Hargreaves, A., 'Dissonant Voices, Dissipated Lives: Teachers and the Multiple Realities of Restructuring', Paper presented at 6th International Conference of ISATT, University of Gothenburg, Sweden, 1993.

Hearn, J., *Men In the Public Eye,* London, Routledge, 1992.

Helterline, M., 'The Emergence of Modern Motherhood: Motherhood in England, 1899–1959', *International Journal of Women's Studies* 3,6, 1980, pp. 590–615.

Hill Collins, P., 'Shifting the Centre: Race, Class and Feminist Theorizing About Motherhood' in Glenn, E., Chang, G. and Forcey, L. (eds), *Mothering: Ideology, Experience and Agency,* New York, Routledge, pp. 45–65, 1994.

Hirsch, M., *The Mother/Daughter Plot: Narrative, Psychoanalysis, Feminism,* Bloomington, Indiana University Press, 1989.

Huberman, M., *The Lives of Teachers,* (trans. J. Neufeld) N.Y. Teachers' College Press / London, Cassells, 1993.

Jaggar, A., 'Love and Knowledge: Emotion in Feminist Epistemology' in Jaggar, A. and Bordo, S. (eds), *Gender / Body / Knowledge: Feminist Reconstructions of Being and Knowing,* New Brunswick, Rutgers University Press, 1989.

Jung, C., *The Portable Jung* (ed. Joseph Campbell), New York, Viking Press, 1971.

Kelly, L., Burton, S. and Regan, L., 'Researching Women's Lives or Studying Women's Oppression? Reflections on What Constitutes Feminist Research' in Maynard, M. and Purvis, J. (eds), *Researching Women's Lives from a Feminist Perspective,* London, Taylor & Francis 1994, pp. 27–48.

King, R., *All Things Bright and Beautiful,* Chichester, James Wiley, 1978.

Kitzinger, S., *The Experience of Childbirth,* 5th edn., Harmondsworth, Penguin, 1984.

Kristeva, J., 'Stabat Mater' in Toril Moi (ed.), *The Kristeva Reader,* Oxford, Basil Blackwell, 1986, pp. 160–86.

Kutnick, P., *Relations in the Primary School Classroom,* London, Paul Chapman, 1988.

Lather, P., 'Research As Praxis', *Harvard Educational Review* 56, 3, 1986, pp. 257–77.

Leach, P., *Baby and Child: From Birth to Age Five,* London, Penguin, 1989.

Levinson, D., with Darrow, C., Klein, G., Levinson, M. and McKee, B., *The Seasons of a Man's Life,* New York, Alfred A. Knopf, 1979.

Lewin, E., 'Negotiating Lesbian Motherhood: The Dialectics of Resistance and Accommodation' in Glenn, E., Chang, G. and Forcey, L. (eds), *Mothering: Ideology, Experience and Agency,* New York, Routledge, 1994, pp. 333–53.

Lewis, C. and O'Brien, M. (eds), *Reassessing Fatherhood: New Observations on Fathers and the Modern Family,* London, Sage, 1987.

Mac an Ghaill, M., *Young, Gifted and Black,* Milton Keynes, Open University, 1988.

Maines, D., 'Narrative's Moment and Sociology's Phenomena: Toward a Narrative Sociology', *Sociological Quarterly* 34, 1, 1993, pp. 17–38.

Martin, J., *Reclaiming a Conversation: The Ideal of the Educated Woman,* New Haven, Yale University Press, 1985.

Maynard, M., 'Feminism and the possibilities of a postmodern research practice', *British Journal of Sociology of Education* 14, 3, 1993, pp. 327–31.

References

Maynard, M. and Purvis, J. (eds), *Researching Women's Lives from a Feminist Perspective*, London, Taylor & Francis, 1994.

Maynard, M. and Purvis, J., 'Doing Feminist Research' in Maynard, M. and Purvis, J. (eds), *Researching Women's Lives from a Feminist Perspective*, London, Taylor & Francis 1994, pp. 1–9.

McKee, L. and O'Brien, M. (eds), *The Father Figure*, London, Tavistock, 1982.

McLaughlin, D. and Tierney, W. (eds), *Naming Silenced Lives: Personal Narratives and Processes of Educational Change*, New York, Routledge, 1993.

Measor, L. and Sikes, P., *Gender and Schools*, London, Cassells, 1992.

Middleton, S., 'Developing A Radical Pedagogy' in Goodson, I. (ed.), *Studying Teachers' Lives*, London, Routledge, 1992.

Morgan, D., *Discovering Men*, London, Routledge, 1992.

Mother & Baby, 'True Love: That Magical Bond With Your Baby', August, 1994, pp. 8–10.

Moustakis, C., *Heuristic Research: Design, Methodology and Applications*, Newbury Park, Sage, 1990.

Nash, C. (ed.), *Narrative in Culture: The Use of Storytelling in the Sciences, Philosophy and Culture*, London, Routledge, 1990.

Neal, S., 'Researching Powerful People from a Feminist and Anti-racist Perspective: A Note on Gender, Collusion and Marginality', *British Educational Research Journal* 21, 4, 1995, pp. 517–31.

Nias, J., *Primary Teachers Talking: A Study of Teaching as Work*, London, Routledge, 1989.

Nielsen, J. (ed.), *Feminist Research Methods, Exemplary Readings in the Social Sciences*, London, Westview Press, 1990.

Oakley, A., *From Here to Maternity: Becoming a Mother*, Harmondsworth, Penguin, 1979.

Oakley, A., 'Interviewing Women – A Contradiction in Terms' in Roberts, H. (ed.), *Doing Feminist Research*, London, Routledge, 1981.

Oakley, A., *Social Support and Motherhood*, Oxford, Basil Blackwell, 1992.

Ostriker, A., *Writing Like a Woman*, Ann Arbor, University of Michigan Press, 1983.

Packwood, A. and Sikes, P., 'Telling Our Stories: Adopting a Post Modern Approach to Research', *International Journal of Qualitative Studies in Education* 9, 3, 1996, pp. 1–11.

Passerini, L., *Fascism in Popular Memory: The Cultural Experience of the Turin Working Class*, Cambridge, Cambridge University Press, 1987.

Patton, M., *Qualitative Evaluation and Research Methods* (2nd ed.), Newbury Park, Sage, 1990.

Personal Narratives Group, *Interpreting Women's Lives: Feminist Theory and Personal Narratives*, Bloomington, Indiana University Press, 1989.

Phoenix, A. and Woollett, A., 'Motherhood: Social Construction, Politics and Psychology' in Phoenix, A., Woollett, A. and Lloyd, E. (eds), *Motherhood: Meanings, Practices and Ideologies*, London, Sage, 1991.

Phoenix, A., Woolett, A. and Lloyd, E. (eds), *Motherhood: Meanings, Practices and Ideologies*, London, Sage, 1991.

Phoenix, A., 'Practising Feminist Research: The Intersection of Gender and 'Race' in the Research Process' in Maynard, M. and Purvis, J. (eds), *Researching Women's Lives from a Feminist Perspective*, London, Taylor & Francis, 1994, pp. 49–71.

Pinar, W., 'The Trial, from Life History and Educational Experience, *Journal of Curriculum Theorizing* 2, 1, 1980, pp. 71–92.

Pinar, W., *Autobiography: Politics and Sexuality: Essays in Curriculum Theory 1972–1992*, New York, Peter Lang, 1994.

Plummer, K., 'Herbert Blumer and the Life History Tradition', *Symbolic Interactionism* 11, 2, 1990, pp. 125–44.

Plummer, K., *Symbolic Interactionism: Volumes 1 and 2*, Aldershot, Edward Elgar Reference, 1991.

Plummer, K., *Telling Sexual Stories: Power, Change and Social Worlds*, London, Routledge, 1995.

Pollard, A., 'A Model of Classroom Coping Strategies', *British Journal of Sociology of Education* 3, 1, 1982, pp. 19–37.

Polyani, M., *The Tacit Dimension*, New York, Doubleday, 1983.

Popular Memory Group, 'Popular Memory: Theory, Politics, Method' in Johnson, R., McLennan, G., Schwarz, B. and Sutton, D. (eds.), *Making Histories*, London, Hutchinson, 1982.

Ramazanoglu, C., 'On Feminist Methodology: Male Reason Vs Female Empowerment', *Sociology* 26, 2, 1992.

Rich, A., *Of Woman Born: Motherhood as Experience and Institution*, London, Virago, 1986.

Rose, G., *Love's Work*, London, Chatto & Windus, 1995.

Rothman, B. K., 'Beyond Mothers and Fathers: Ideology in a Patriarchal Society' in Glenn, E.N., Chang, G. and Forcey, L.R., *Mothering: Ideology, Experience and Agency*, London, Routledge, 1994.

Ruddick, S., 'Maternal Thinking' in Treblicott, J. (ed.), *Mothering: Essays in Feminist Theory*, Maryland, Rowman & Littlefield, 1983.

Sikes, P., 'The Life Cycle of the Teacher' in Ball, S. and Goodson, I. (eds), *Teachers' Lives and Careers*, Lewes, Falmer, 1985, pp. 27–60.

Sikes, P., Measor, L. and Woods, P., *Teacher Careers: Crises and Continuities*, Lewes, Falmer, 1985.

Sikes, P. and Troyna, B., 'True Stories: A Case Study in the Use of Life History in Initial Teacher Education', *Educational Review* 43, 1, 1991, pp. 3–16.

Sikes, P. and Aspinwall, K., 'Time to Reflect: Biographical Study, Personal Insight and Professional Development' in Young, A. and Collin, R. (eds), *Interpreting Career: Hermeneutical Studies of Lives in Context*, Westport, Connecticut, Praeger, 1992.

Sikes, P., Troyna, B. and Goodson, I., 'Talking About Teachers: A Conversation About Life History', *Taboo: The Journal of Culture and Education*, Vol. 1, Spring, 1996, pp. 35–54.

Smart, C., *The Ties That Bind: Law, Marriage and the Reproduction of Patriarchal Relations*, London, Routledge & Kegan Paul, 1984.

Sparkes, A., 'Physical Education Teachers and the Search for Self: Two Cases of Structured Denial' in Armstrong, N. (ed.), *New Directions in Physical Education*, Vol. 3, London, Cassells, 1995.

Spelman, E., *Inessential Woman: Problems of Exclusion in Feminist Thought*, Boston, Beacon Press, 1988.

Stanley, L., *Feminist Praxis, Research, Theory and Epistemology in Feminist Sociology*, London, Routledge, 1990.

Stanley, L. and Wise, S., *Breaking Out Again: Feminist Ontology and Epistemology*, London, Routledge, 1983.

Steedman, C., *The Tidy House*, London, Virago, 1982.

Steedman, C., *Landscape For A Good Woman: A Story of Two Lives*, London, Virago, 1986.

Steedman, C., Urwin, C. and Walkerdine, V. (eds), *Language, Gender and Childhood*, London, Routledge & Kegan Paul, 1985.

Steedman, C., 'Prisonhouses' in Lawn, M. and Grace, G. (eds), *Teachers: The Culture and Politics of Work*, Lewes, Falmer, 1987.

Steedman, C., 'The Mother Made Conscious: The Historical Development of a Primary School Pedagogy' in Woodhead, M. and McGrath, A. (eds), *Family, School and Society*, Milton Keynes, Open University Press, 1988.

Tierney, W., 'Self and Identity in a Post-modern world: A Life Story' in McLaughlin, D. and Tierney, W. (eds), *Naming Silenced Lives: Personal Narratives and Processes of Educational Change*, New York, Routledge, 1993, pp. 119–34.

Treblicot, J. (ed.), *Mothering: Essays in Feminist Theory*, Maryland, Rowman & Littlefield, 1983.

References

Troyna, B., 'Blind Faith? Empowerment and Educational Research', *International Studies in the Sociology of Education* 4, 1, 1994, pp. 3–24.

Troyna, B., 'Reforms, Research and Being Reflexive About Being Reflexive' in Halpin, D. and Troyna, B. (eds), *Researching Educational Policy: Ethical and Methodological Issues*, London, Falmer, 1994.

Tyler, D., 'Setting the Child Free': Teachers, Mothers and Child-Centered Pedagogy in the 1930's Kindergarten' in Blackmore, J. and Kenway, J. (eds), *Gender Matters in Educational Administration and Policy: A Feminist Introduction*, Falmer, London, 1993.

Urwin, C., 'Constructing Motherhood: The Persuasion of Normal Development' in Steedman, C., Urwin, C. and Walkerdine, V. (eds), *Language, Gender and Childhood*, London, Routledge & Kegan Paul, 1985.

Van Maanan, J., *Tales of the Field*, Chicago, University of Chicago Press, 1988.

Ve, H., 'The Male Gender Role and Responsibility for Children' in Boh, K. et al (eds), *Changing Patterns of European Family Life*, London, Routledge, 1989, pp. 249 –63.

Walkerdine, V., 'Post-Structuralist Theory and Everyday Social Practices: The Family and the School' in Wilkinson, S. (ed.), *Feminist Social Psychology: Development, Theory and Practice*, Milton Keynes, Open University Press, 1986.

Walkerdine, V. and Lucey, H., *Democracy in the Kitchen: Regulating Mothers and Socialising Daughters*, London, Virago, 1989.

Wilkins, R., 'Taking it Personally: A Note on Emotions and Autobiography', *Sociology* 27, 1, 1993, pp. 93–100.

Withering, C. and Nodding, N. (eds), *Stories Lives Tell: Narrative and Dialogue in Education*, Columbia New York, Teachers' College Press, 1991, pp. 67–77.

Wittgenstein, L., *Philosophical Investigations* (3rd edn), trans. G. Anscombe) New York, Macmillan, 1968, original work published in 1953.

Woods, P., *The Divided School*, London, Routledge & Kegan Paul, 1979.

Yates, P., *The Fun Starts Here: A Practical Guide to the Bliss of Babies*, London, Bloomsbury, 1990.

Index

teaching
  as a profession for women 62–4, 103
  role of mothers in 50–2, 138–9
  see also pedagogy
testing children at school 71
theory, educational 12, 68–9, 74, 79, 109
time off to care for sick children 138
Times Educational Supplement xvii–xviii
tolerance 73, 135
'traditional values' 56, 69
training of teachers 68–9, 72, 74, 98, 109,
  121, 135
  advisory panel on 106
transformational experience,
  motherhood as 1
triangulation techniques 25
Troyna, B. 18
truth, nature of 19, 25, 136
Tyler, D. 80

union activities 106
unitary view of the person 136
Urwin, C. *see* Steedman, Carolyn *et al*

valuing of nurture and care 141
Van Maanan, J. xvii
vanity-led research 2, 18
'verisimilitude' xviii
verstehen, concept of 30
vocabulary, parent teachers' 26, 30

Walkerdine, V. 80, *see also* Steedman,
  Carolyn *et al*
whole child, the, development of 69–70
Wittgenstein, L. xvii
women academics, writing of xv–xvi
Woods, Peter xvii
working-class background and attitudes 58,
  68, 80, 83, 88, 97–9, 105, 110, 125
working mothers (in general) 9–10, 47, 64,
  100, 106, 108
world-view, shared 5, 7, 69, 95, 134
Wright Mills, C. 1

Yates, Paula 48

zeitgeist 53, 69

South East Essex College
of Arts & Technology
Carnarvon Road Southend-on-Sea Essex SS2 6LS
Tel: (01702) 220400 Fax: (01702) 432320 Minicom: (01702) 220642